Wayne Grind

LOYALTY, LOVE,

& BETRAYAL

SURVIVING THE HAND THAT WAS DEALT
GROWING UP IN THE HOOD

PART ONE

WRITTEN BY

WAYNE GRIND

Wayne Grind

LOYALTY, LOVE,

& BETRAYAL

SURVIVING THE HAND THAT WAS DEALT
GROWING UP IN THE HOOD

PART ONE

WRITTEN BY

WAYNE GRIND

Wayne Grind

PRAISE FOR:

LOYALTY, LOVE, & BETRAYAL

SURVIVING THE HAND THAT WAS DEALT GROWING UP IN THE HOOD
PART ONE

WRITTEN BY
WAYNE GRIND

"After reading "Loyalty, Love, & BETRAYAL" by author Wayne Grind, I feel he may be the next go-to author for urban hood stories. His book is full of twist and turns, and great tales of really surviving the hand that was dealt to young, black youth in the ghetto street-life, and having the ability to overcome such obstacles and tough situations. Putting it on paper is a great accomplishment. I highly recommend that you get your copy!"
- Kelsey Nykole: Artist/Songwriter/VH1 Star

"Wayne Grind's new book "Loyalty, Love, & BETRAYAL "is raw, gritty, and extremely real. Once he put his heart on paper with pen, his unique, edgy, and gripping story of growing up in the hood, full of Loyalty, Love, & BETRAYAL, was born. It is real, and I appreciate him sharing this story with the world. I wish you much success and may God be with you, Wayne. I highly recommend this book."
- King J. Harden: Singer/Songwriter/ Entrepreneur - kingjharden.com

"I personally know Wayne Grind as a hard worker, a street guy, and an author and businessman. I can say that this great urban hood story is a must-read. Wayne does a great job of painting a realistic picture of what

Wayne Grind

it is like growing up as a young, black man with a hard-core street life and with limited options. The title and cover depict the book at its best. From the first page to the last page, I highly recommend Wayne Grind's book which is full of Loyalty, Love, & BETRAYAL. He kept it real while clearly describing what it's like to grow up in the hood."
- Heartbeatz: Producer/Songwriter

"Loyalty, Love, & BETRAYAL: Surviving the Hand that was Dealt Growing Up in the Hood - Part 1" by Wayne Grind has a great mix of truth, rawness, grit, and survival about growing up in the hard-core urban neighborhoods and projects of New Orleans, along with discovery, coming-of-age, dealing with good or bad situations, forgiveness, betrayal, family ties, and love. This story is pure, and encompasses a very realistic picture of life on the streets, gang life, prison life and poverty. It also is about overcoming the harshest conditions and challenges one can face, and learning how to stay strong and make something of one's life. Author Wayne Grind bravely puts his heart, soul and truths into this book, and it is definitely a must-read."
- Suzanne Sumner Ferry: Author (*The Day the Stars Stood Still*, 2012; *Corinna the Christmas Elf*, 2009)/Actor/Producer/Screenwriter/CEO, FERRY PRODUCTIONS, INC. suzanne.ferry@verizon.net, suzannesferry.com

LOOK for LOYALTY, LOVE,

& BETRAYAL

SURVIVING THE HAND THAT WAS DEALT GROWING UP IN THE HOOD

PART TWO

BY AUTHOR WAYNE GRIND - **COMING SOON!**

A FATHER'S PAIN...

R.I.P. JUAN

© 2010 Duane Brannon

Wayne Grind

Loyalty, Love, & BETRAYAL: Surviving the Hand that was Dealt Growing Up in the Hood - Part One

Copyright © 2016 by Wayne Grind.

www.waynegrindpublishing.com

Edited by Suzanne Sumner Ferry, Actor/Producer/Author (*The Day the Stars Stood Still -* Copyright © 2012 by Suzanne Sumner Ferry; *Corinna the Christmas Elf* - Copyright © 2009 by Suzanne Sumner Ferry)

CEO, FERRY PRODUCTIONS, INC. - suzanne.ferry@verizon.net - suzannesferry.com

First Edition

ISBN-978-0-692-27561-0

Published and Printed in the United States of America

Copyright © 2016 Cover design and layout: INMOTION MEDIA
Copyright © 2010 Interior Artwork "A Father's Grief" by Duane Brannon

10 9 8 7 6 5 4 3 2 1

DEDICATION
&
IN MEMORIAM

To my Moms, Pops, Kim, Elmer, Mommy Nett, RIP Juan (my son), my brother Russell, & Pun Pun...May God bless y'all soul and I pray that y'all rest in peace...Since y'all been gone it's been a constant everyday struggle, but I refuse to give up, I do this for y'all...Love y'all from earth to heaven. RIP Robert Earl, and RIP Doublecup King Naski.

Wayne Grind

SPECIAL THANKS

To my friend and my partner who motivated me to pursue my dreams fulltime, who consulted and guided me through some tough situations, and who gave me the name Wayne Grind: We fuss, we fight, but together we stick when it is time to get the job done. Thank you, Ms. Joe'i Chancellor.

I would like to thank my editor and friend, Suzanne Sumner Ferry. I swear Ms. Ferry came into my life at a point where I was on the verge of giving up on putting out my book. So many people cheated me out of money for services which they never provided. However, Suzanne has kept her word 100% from day one. After working on my story, I knew she has believed in me the entire time, and has shown me kindness till the end. Suzanne, you are truly a Godsend, and I can't thank you or pay you enough for the love you have shown. I love working with you. We have one book down, and (at least) two to go!

I also want to thank Mrs. Janice Brumfield for her love and support, for sticking with me, and staying up for days and nights working on my book...I want you to know that you may not think you mean anything to the world, but you mean the world to me. You are one of my angels, and I can't thank you enough.

A big shout-out to Mr. Joe Cleezy and to Floyd for your support, and for staying down with a nigga through it ALL...your help with everything is real, and very much appreciated.

ACKNOWLEDGEMENTS

I would like to start by giving God Almighty the glory and praise for keeping a nobody like myself, giving me the opportunity to turn my negatives into positives, and allowing me to make something of myself. I love you, Father, for your love and grace. There were certain situations that some people never understood how I could overcome them. Sometimes I didn't understand it myself, but I know that it was you, Heavenly Father, who stuck beside me when everyone else fled from strife. It was only you who protected me, so it's only you whom I will praise. I thank you; I thank you; Amen.

I would like to thank my sisters, my brothers, my nieces, nephews, aunts, uncles, cousins, and friends who kept me in prayers when I was lost, thuggin', drugging, and incarcerated. Thanks to all those who stood beside me, whether up or down. You know who you are. Love y'all.

I want to give a big shout-out to my grandson, my kids, and my baby mothers for honestly putting up with my B.S., and my being away. It may seem a little selfish at times, but it took great sacrifices to get this book done. Thank y'all for never giving up on me and sticking by my side, and loving me anyway. I love y'all to pieces for that.

I give a big thanks to my ex-wife for holding me down, and being a soldier in my time of need for your support. I admit that incarceration detached me from emotions, which caused me to fail at returning love. With that being said, I apologize for us not makin' it. I wish you the best that life has to offer you and your love ones. And to all my exes: thanks for the experiences, and even though we didn't make it, I learned from every situation.

Wayne Grind

   Thanks to all the people who wish to see me succeed; thanks to all who wish to see me fail, LOL. I see y'all who are straddling the fence to see if I'm gonna win or lose, to see which way y'all are gonna rock. For years, I took your love for granted, not really appreciating the woman you are, nor the love and companionship that you tried to share with me. Right or wrong, you were my ride or die. But now we travel through life on different paths, with different people, and I still pray that God blesses and protects you with love and peace. The memories we share can never be wiped away, and you are forever my friend.

   I want thank the two niggas I did my first everything with, who taught me the streets, survival, and women. FREE Jaime Gat and Seafood; love y'all. I hope the future holds better days for you both. FREE my brother Ricky. Man, I can't explain how much I miss you. Just know I'm here for you until you touch down. To my cousin, Booty Earl. Man, I wish you woulda listened to me. But regardless, I'm gonna hold it down. I do it for y'all.

   I want to thank my beautiful mother, and my hardworking father, both of whom are deceased. Thank you both for giving birth to me, loving me, and protecting me in this cruel world until death did us part. R.I.P. to both of you. I want to thank my mom for instilling me with church values, respect, and manners, before leaving this earth. I also want to apologize to Pops for thinking you were too hard on me. Pops, as I look back on life, I must admit that the tough love you gave has really prepared me to stand as a man today. It was all worth it. I just hate that it took me to go through hell and the places I went, to understand that you were only trying to do your fatherly duties and raise your child.

-Wayne Grind

INTRODUCTION

Loyalty, Love, & BETRAYAL is a great urban hood story about young kids growing up in the city streets, adapting quickly to the street life and having the privilege to be schooled by an old gangsta by the name of Silk. Silk preached all the time about the coldness of this world, and the game. But after Silk was hospitalized from a gunshot wound, the gang was worried and disappointed. It showed on their faces. Silk was like a father to them, and things just weren't the same without going to Silk's car wash, soaking up the game, and making that money. Champ and the gang were confused about what had happened to Silk, but then the good news came that Silk had made it out. However, things would never be the same around the shop again. "Survival by Any Means" became the gang's motto...in or out...and Silk needed them. They were family.

This book is real. It is a must-read.

Wayne Grind

LOYALTY, LOVE, & BETRAYAL

SURVIVING THE HAND THAT WAS DEALT GROWING UP IN THE HOOD

PART ONE

WRITTEN BY

WAYNE GRIND

Wayne Grind

CHAPTER ONE

The sound of his mama being beaten by his pop every night during his youth was something that Champ will never forget. As he beat her, she would scream, and as she screamed, Champ would lie in his bed staring at the ceiling...just listening to it. In the beginning, it would aggravate him. He would try to block out the sound by covering his head with a pillow. It became so regular that it didn't bother him. He ate with it, slept with it, and lived with it every single day.

It was the summer of '81 and all the kids were out of school. While the other kids were going to camps or some fantastic theme parks, Champ's summer was usually spent just in the neighborhood, out on his block. His mom was a very nice lady, and even though she didn't have a job, whenever she talked to him she would always say, "Everything that I do, it's only to make you happy." Champ thought that's why his next-door neighbor, Mr. Henry, would always sneak in the back door when his Pops was away. He would always see him do it from his bedroom window. Moms would let him in and they'd lock up in her room, and wouldn't come out for hours. Sometimes, Champ would put his ear to the door and listen. He would always hear his mom inside, yelling and making some weird noises. One day he cracked the door open to see what was going on in there and saw Mr. Henry and his Mom in the bed, butt-naked.

Pops was kind of a nice fella although he wouldn't talk very much. He was always working or hanging out with his buddy, Leroy. When they did talk, he would ask Champ, "Champ, have you found you a squeeze or a sponge?"

Champ would always giggle and reply, "Nope."

Champ used to always wonder why Pops went to work clean and came home clean. Every weekend Moms would iron his uniforms for the whole week, and Champ would shine all of his shoes. He enjoyed that because then he could play "Jungle Man" because they all looked like snakes and alligators. He'd always give Champ a two-dollar bill to put in his pocket, but Moms would take it and give him two dollars in change. She always said that a two-dollar bill was good luck.

Every now and then, Pops would take Champ riding with him in his pretty car. He never knew the name of it, but Pops used to call it "Eldog." He would take his son across this long bridge and pick up this lady named Ms. Katt and her two kids. Then they would go straight to Chuck E. Cheese's to eat pizza and play games. Ms. Katt's son, Bo, was the same age as Champ, and her daughter Holly was a few years older than they were. They would leave the kids at Chuck E. Cheese's and tell Holly to keep an eye on the boys. During that time, Champ felt that he really began to live. It was June 8, 1981.

Champ remembered one time when his Pops took him over to Ms. Katt's house to stay for the weekend. He always wondered why her son's bedroom was the same as his. He even had the same clothes and toys as Champ did. For most of the day, he and Bo played with the toys inside while Holly talked on the phone to boys. Toward the end of the day they walked to Ms. Katt's bedroom, stood in the doorway, and watched her as she got dressed to go out and have a good time. Ms. Katt was so fine. At first, she didn't even notice Champ standing there as she pulled her silk stockings up her sexy pair of legs. When she did turn around to see Champ, she looked surprised. She grabbed a pair of clip-on earrings off her dresser and began putting them on her ears while saying, "Hey Champ, baby, what's wrong? Are you bored?"

He shook his head from side-to-side and replied, "Naw, I was just thinking about something."

As she reached down to grab a pair of high-heeled pumps from the foot of her bed, she asked, "What were you thinking about?"

He walked over to her bed, sat on it, and asked her, "How come everything that I got at my house, Bo has here?"

Ms. Katt was so shocked at what Champ had asked that she stopped what she was doing and looked at him through the mirror on her dresser. She couldn't find a good enough answer, so he continued by asking her, "Why do Pops buy Bo everything that he buy me?"

She stood silent for a moment before saying, "Now baby, who said that your daddy bought those things?"

All of a sudden, Bo stepped into her bedroom doorway and said, "I did, Mamma. It was me who told him that!"

Ms. Katt looked at Champ, then at Bo. She took a deep breath, closed her eyes, and said, "Look! I'm about to go out and have myself a good time. I'll talk to y'all later about this!" Then she turned toward the mirror and began putting some makeup on her face. "Now y'all go tell Holly to get y'all some cookies off the shelf!" Neither of them moved.

She turned around and looked at both of them and said, "This ain't the time and I ain't the one to tell you, so will you please be good and wait until tomorrow and I'll have y'all da--" she stopped because she realized that she was about to say something that she wasn't supposed to. When a car horn blew outside, she hurried and grabbed her purse. "Look, y'all! Be good, okay?"

"Alright, Momma," Holly replied. Then Ms. Katt left.

After Ms. Katt left, the boys stayed up watching an old gangsta movie called *The Cotton Club*. However, after what had gone on in Ms. Katt's bedroom, Bo and Champ had very little to say to each other, if anything at all. The rest of the night was pretty much the same. The gangsta movie went off and they fell asleep in the middle of an old *Laurel and Hardy* clipping.

The next morning was a total wreck. Ms. Katt walked into Bo's room with her nightgown on, Holly right behind her, and said, "Champ, baby? How come you don't want to eat breakfast?"

He replied, "I want to go home!"

"There are a lot of kids around here for you to play with if that's yo' problem," she said. But he continued to say that he wanted to go home.

"Well. I'll just call your daddy and have him come and pick you up," she said as she left the room. When she left, Bo walked into the room with the exact same Super Friends pajamas that Champ had on Saturday, which were lying on the other end of the bed across from him.

As he sat on the bed all frowned up, he asked, "Champ, man, how come you want to go home? Today we were supposed to go outside and play football with my friends."

Champ replied, "Nigga! Why you worried about me so much? Shoot!" he continued, raising his voice, "People don't like it over here!" Champ ranted on more, "Y'all ain't kin to me anyway, and besides, I got my own friends that I can play with!"

Bo got up off the bed and yelled, "See how much you know! My Daddy already told us that he brought you over here to play with me because they wasn't any kids your age around your house!"

"Nigga, you lying!" Champ shouted abruptly.

"Yeah, he did!" Bo shouted.

"And, nigga, that *ain't* your Daddy!" Champ screamed.

"Yeah, he is, bitch!" Bo yelled.

That's when Champ got up off the bed, balled his fists up and shouted, "Nigga, you a bitch!"

Bo balled up his fists as well and replied, "I betcha' I can kick your fuckin' ass!" and then they both ran toward each other and started fighting. He decked Champ in the nose, and Champ punched him in his eye.

They kept fighting until Holly came running into the room yelling, "Momma! Momma! They fightin' up in here!"

Ms. Katt rushed into the room and they broke them up. Bo said, as she held him by the collar of his PJ's, "He started it, Momma!"

"Bitch, you started it!" Champ shouted.

Ms. Katt looked at Champ astounded, and said, "Oh, no! Champ baby, you got to go with all that cussin' cause my children don't be doing no cussing!" As she shoved Bo out of the room, she said "Holly, come out of there and close that door. Leave his ass in there until his daddy comes to get him."

Holly walked to the door, then looked back and said, "Yo' daddy gon' whoop you, boy!"

"Get outta here, bitch!" Champ yelled.

She slammed the door shut. Nothing was going to happen to him until Pops came. It took him a while to get there. In fact, it took him so long that Champ fell asleep waiting for him. He must've slept for about an hour before he felt someone shaking him to wake up. It was Pops. Champ recognized his voice as he continued to say, "Champ, wake up! Champ, wake up!"

Champ woke up, wiped his eyes, looked at Pops, and quickly said to him "Man, I'm ready to go home. I don't like it out here!"

Pops and Champ had a long talk, for about a half hour or more. He was mainly talking to Champ about his attitude. He kept reminding his son about what he had told him before; how to act around friends of his. He would always say that he would never bring Champ by someone he didn't trust. Then he called Bo into the room and talked to them both. He told them that they were closer than they thought. The reason why Bo had everything that Champ had was because he was his blood brother. The boys both found it sort of funny when Pops said, "Y'all both fell from the same Walnut tree, but just on a different lawn."

That's when Champ said, "But I thought you loved me?" He looked Pops in his eyes, desperately waiting for his answer.

"I do, Champ!" he replied, as he placed his hands on Champ's shoulder. "I love you both," he said. "That's why everything I buy, I buy it for two. And by the way, y'all didn't make me mad by fighting with each other."

They both replied at the same time, "You ain't mad?"

Pops shook his head from side to side and said, "If y'all don't fight the outsiders then I'm going to be mad, y'all understand?" They both nodded their heads. Then Pops looked at Champ and said, "Now, Champ, I want you to go in there and apologize to Katt." Champ stared at Pops for a moment with a frown on his face. He knew that he didn't want to go in there and tell her that he was sorry, but he knew he had to.

Bo looked at him and said, "Go 'head bro, don't be scared." Champs looked at him, then at Pops. He got up and headed to her bedroom to apologize. He was only nine at the time and that seemed like the hardest thing for him to do. He slowly walked into Ms. Katt's bedroom where she stood with her back turned toward him while making up her bed. He was too embarrassed to say a word so he just stood there silently with his back against the wall staring at her. She started to the other side of the bed when she noticed Champ standing there.

"You always sneaking up on me, huh?" she asked, as she continued making the bed. After a few moments, she turned to Champ and asked, "So, did your daddy send you up here to tell me something?" Champ just stood there and said nothing as she continued making up her bed. Then she said, "Well, whenever you get ready, I'll be here." She finally looked up at him but he kept his head down, too ashamed to speak. After she pulled the last crease out of the bedspread and took a look just to be sure that the bed was properly made, she looked over to where he was standing, only to see that he had left the room. She spoke in a low tone to herself saying, "He so mannish."

She then went to her dresser to clean it up a bit. It was only a few moments before Champ came back into the room with his head still hanging down and said, "Ms. Katt, I am sorry for cussing in front of you today."

She walked over to where he was and stooped down to look him in the eyes and said, "Champ, baby, listen. I know it is hard being around a woman other than your momma, but I love you like you was my own." She continued, "I know that I can never take her place, but anything that you need that she can't give you, you just call me, okay?" Champ nodded his head and that was it. He found out that it wasn't so hard after all.

After that was over, the boys ate breakfast and then went outside to play with Bo's friends. They were already outside playing. One kid was playing with a spinning top in an empty lot where all the kids in the neighborhood did most of their playing. Bo yelled at him, "Hey, Dusty, come here!"

When he came over, Champ realized that he was younger than they were. Bo asked him, "Where your brother at, nigga?"

Dusty looked at Bo with a strange look and said, "They all went to the clubhouse, bra. Who this nigga is?"

Bo replied, "Stop worrying about that you Lil' bad mutha fucka!"

"Aw, fuck you, nigga!" Dusty replied, as they all started toward the clubhouse. They walked across the empty lot to a fence that had a hole in it. They climbed through the hole and ended up in the yard of an abandoned apartment complex. There was trash and debris everywhere. Most of the windows were boarded up so that vandals couldn't get in. They came to a rather long alley which lined one side of the property, and a kid was sitting up in a big Chinese Elm tree. He said, "Nigga, you late!"

Bo looked up at the kid and said, "Man, I had to go somewhere with my Pops. Donkey, come down from there. I got somebody I want everybody to meet." Donkey started climbing down out of the tree.

Bo looked at his brother and said, "Say, Champ, do you like dogs?"

Champ replied, "Yes I do, very much so!"

At the end of the alley, the last apartment they had set up as a clubhouse. Bo opened the door and they all went in. Inside, two other boys were sitting on a raggedy sofa playing with some small Pitbull puppies. They both looked at Bo with an angry look, and he knew that they were mad because he hadn't showed up on time. So he told them that their Pops had come and picked him up, and then one of the boys stood up and said "Man, you getting worse than Bruce with that shit!"

"Don't say that!" Bruce said. "Cause I haven't been late in a while."

That's when Bo said, "Busty, my brother wants in!"

All the kids in the clubhouse yelled at the same time, "What?"

Finally, Busty broke the silence and said, "Man, you ain't told us you had a brother." Then Bo told them that he and Champ had the same daddy.

Champ finally relaxed when Bo walked over and picked up one of the puppies and said, "Champ, meet the gang."

Bo walked over to the first boy they saw in the lot and started introducing his brother to the gang. "This is Dusty, the baby thief of the gang," and they all started giggling.

He walked over to Donkey and described him as a 'pretty boy' and Donkey replied, "Girls just love me."

Then he walked over to Bruce and said, "This is Big Bruce."

Right then is when Dusty said, "The fat motherfucker." Dusty
began to laugh until Bo gave him a strange look, and he shut up.

He walked over to Busty and said, "He is half of the mind that keeps this gang together and tight." Then he said, "Gang, meet Champ; my brother."

Champ looked at everyone for a few seconds, nodding his head up and down repeatedly. He was in a gang. Right then he knew one thing...that he was going to like it over there after all. For the next few days, he hung out with the gang. Champ was having the best time of his life.

One day, Bruce asked Champ when he was planning on going home. Champ told him that he was going to ask Pops if he could stay for the rest of the summer. They all began to smile and cheer, and that's when the little guy they called Dusty said, "Then you can come and work with us, man!"

Champ looked around at everybody and asked, "What is he talking about?"

It was silent for a few seconds as everybody looked at each other and then Busty finally said, "Say, bro, one weekend we go to the car wash and do a few jobs for a few nickels and dimes and stuff. But, umm...you can stay here if you don't want to come." They all looked at Champ, waiting to hear his response.

He looked at Bo and said, "If the gang wash cars, then I wash cars!" and they all smiled.

At the end of the day, the gang went home and when Champ arrived back to Ms. Katt's house, he went into her bedroom. She was watching television. He asked her if she knew if his dad was going to pass over there today.

She looked at Champ and replied, "I can call him if you want me to, but he will be coming over here tonight to pick you up. Why? You ready to go home now?"

Champ turned to look at the television and then back at her and said, "I don't want to go home." She was astounded, and then she asked him how long he wanted to stay. He looked her directly in her eyes and said, "For the rest of the summer." She cracked a big smile.

That night when Pops came to bring Champ home, he told Pops that he wanted to stay for the summer. He just looked at his son with this crazy look on his face. Champ guessed that the talk that he had with Pops had brought a sudden change, but it wasn't the talk with him that did it. It would probably fall in the category of freedom. Champ never had friends before and now that he did, he thought he'd stay for a while. Of course, Pops would get in a big argument with his Mom once he told her about it. Yet, with Champ knowing Pops as he did, he knew he had a way of handling everything.

Champ wanted to know what the gang did at the car wash. The day finally came for them to work. The car wash was only a few blocks away from the clubhouse. When they made it there, it was packed with cars. The whole gang was thinking, *Wow!*

Then Bo said, "Y'all, we about to get paid big time!"

As they got closer, an older guy yelled, "Where have y'all been? These people won't let anybody wash their cars but y'all!"

Busty replied, "You told us to be here at noon."

He looked at all the cars parked at the car wash and said, "Yeah! Yeah! Silk made a mistake. Go ahead and get to work." The gang all headed toward this room where they kept all of their supplies.

The older guy by the name of Silk was a tall, slender fella who wore a dark gray khaki outfit with a nametag that read "Auto Detailing." He was in his thirties, and well-groomed with French braids running down his back. He raised his left hand up to rub his light goatee as he watched the gang scramble through the car wash. Then he noticed Champ. He was helping Bruce fill up the pails for the cars. He knew that there was only five of them, and now six, so he asked, "Who this is?"

The rest of the gang froze and looked at Silk, who then said to them, "Where did he come from?"

"Th-th-that's Bo's brother," Bruce stuttered.

Silk looked Champ directly in his eyes and his knees were shaking like a '66 Mustang in the Indy 500. Silk knew that Champ was nervous and then he asked, "What's your name, Lil' man?" as he started to rub his goatee again.

He said, "My name is Champ."

Then Silk looked over at Bo and said, "To be honest, you do look like that knucklehead."

Then the gang started laughing. He looked back at Champ and asked him if he knew how to wash cars. Champ looked over at Bo who was nodding his head, trying to tell him to say 'yes' and that's when Champ looked back at Silk and said, "Nah!"

All of a sudden, someone yelled across the lot and said, "Say Silk, send them boys over here!" But the gang never moved. They all just stared at Silk in suspense.

Then Silk yelled at all of the boys, "Get to work and show Lil' man here how to wash cars."

As the gang started to wash cars, Silk decided to take Champ over to a long, black Continental that was parked under the third cover, and did a little car washing of his own to show Champ how it was done. He helped Champ wash, rinse, and dry the car. The only part he figured that he would really need to be taught was how to wax the car. Silk carefully showed him how to wax in a way that he wouldn't waste any wax. After they were finished, he stood about five feet away from the car and said, "Come here, Lil' man!" When Champ did, Silk put his arm around Champ's shoulder and said, "For the first time you did kind of good, huh?"

Champ replied, "Yeah!" There wasn't a spot on the Continental. You could see your reflection on the paint job, true spokes, as well as on the vogue tires.

He said, "Okay, do you know what you need to do now?

Champ said, "What?" and Silk pointed over to a crowd of fellas who sat at a table, a good distance away. They were smoking and drinking. Silk asked Champ, "Do you see that fat mutha fucka over there?"

Champ asked, "With the jerry curl?"

"Yeah, Yeah." Silk replied. Then Silk told Champ, "Go over there and tell him to break you off."

When Champ approached the table, one guy asked, "Yeah, Lil' man, what's up?"

Champ looked at the fat guy and said, "Is that your car over there?" He pointed towards the Continental.

The fat guy peeped at his car and saw that it was sparkling and said, "Yes, that is mine. Why?"

He looked at him and said, "I am finished with it," and then all the guys looked at it and sighed.

"Nah! Man, nah!" he yelled. Champ thought something was wrong.

He looked puzzled and then one of the fellas asked, "Champ, is that what Slim told you to come over here and say?"

Champ replied, "Yep!"

Then another fella said, "This Lil' nigga lying his ass off! Come on, Lil' man. Did he really tell you to say that?"

Champ looked at the fat guy then at the other one and said, "Nope."

The fat guy said, "So tell me what he told you to say."

Champ looked at him and said, "He told me to tell you to break me off." The fat guy just stared at him for a few minutes and Champ's knees started shaking again. It was quiet for a moment.

Then the fat guy asked, "Is that all?"

Champ continued by saying, "And for you to break him off, too!"

Then one of the guys said, "I like that, Lil' nigga. House, break him off!" as he did so he told the others that he liked Champ, too.

The guy said, "He a little shady, but he cool." Then he dug in his pocket and pulled out a big bankroll, opened it up and pulled out a five-dollar bill and handed it to Champ. He said, "This is for you." Then he pulled out a ten-dollar bill and handed it to Champ. He said, "This is for the car." He pulled out a twenty, a ten, and a five, and handed them to him and said, "This is for Silky."

Champ took the money and walked over to Silk's office where he sat behind a desk counting some money. He tossed the money on the desk in front of Silk. Silk picked up the money and asked him, "How much is this?" But Champ never said a word.

He looked at Champ for a moment or two then handed the money to him slowly, "Here, count it" he said. Without grabbing the money he looked at it, and then at Silk.

Champ grabbed the money out of his hand and sorted it as Silk looked on. He put the twenty on top, then the two tens, then the two fives and then looked at Silk; and without looking at the money he counted it as he flipped it, saying, "Twenty, thirty, forty, forty-five, and fifty." Then he tossed the money on the desk.

Silk looked at Champ for a moment, then grabbed a five from the money, and said, "He gave this to you, right?" and he handed the five to him. "Now, you can go on out there."

Champ turned and walked out of the office. Silk stared at him as he left, mostly because he was surprised. He had thought that Champ couldn't count, but Champ showed him otherwise.

CHAPTER TWO

You know something? I pretty much liked my first day at the car wash, Champ thought to himself. He had fun while washing the cars; there was music playing, and they got tips for washing the cars. A guy, whose car he washed named Jon Jon, gave him a twenty-dollar tip for his work. There were four sexy ladies in the car with Jon Jon. They all gave Champ a kiss on the cheek because they thought that he was cute and at the end of the day, Silk gave all of the boys fifteen bucks as their day's pay. Champ felt like the richest kid on earth because he had made himself thirty-five dollars in tips plus his fifteen dollars. The first thing Champ wanted to do was to buy himself some All-Stars. But the gang told him to save his money, because it would be a day or two before Silk could pick him up a pair from the shoe store. The day was over and they all went home.

At home, Ms. Katt had cooked some Kraft Macaroni and Cheese with fried chicken for dinner. Champ and Bo ate dinner, took baths, and chilled out. They usually played Atari games after dinner but they were a bit tired that day. At around eight o'clock, the phone rang and Ms. Katt picked it up in her room. She called out to Bo and told him that the phone was for him. It was his girlfriend, Minnie. He brought the phone into his room, took the receiver from his mouth and asked, "You want a girlfriend, Champ?"

A big smile came over Champ's face as he replied, "Yeah!"

Bo handed him the phone. "Here, talk to her," he said.

Champ grabbed the phone and said, "Hello?"

There was a girl on the phone who asked, "Who is this?" When Champ looked at Bo he was standing in front of the dresser, silently showing him that she was eleven with big titties.

He answered, "This is Champ."

"How old are you?" she asked. He told her that he was eleven. He glanced at Bo as he covered up his face and dove onto the bed, trying to stifle his laugh.

"What school do you go to?" she asked.

Then Champ heard a girl in the background asking, "Is he cute, girl?"

He replied, "I am probably going to a school around here next year." He was not sure yet, since his mom didn't know about Ms. Katt yet, but he was hopeful. Then he asked her what school she went to and why she wanted to know where he would be attending.

"I go to a Catholic school," she replied. Then Bo whispered and told Champ that she had a boyfriend named Damian, and that he was in the sixth grade.

So Champ asked her if she had a boyfriend and she yelled, "Tell Bo to shut up, because I don't even go with him anymore!"

"You don't act like Bo, huh?" he asked her.

"How do Bo act?" she countered.

"He nasty!" Champ replied and started laughing. Bo and he talked on the phone with those girls all night, and eventually she told Champ that she would be his girlfriend. That was cool with him. The next day when they went to work, Bo told the gang that Champ and Minnie's sister, Kay, were going together. They all seemed astounded.

Bruce said, "So what! She ain't going to give him no booty because I'm telling you now, she be playing hard to get and stuff."

Busty said, "Nigga, shut up! Because you and Shantel don't be doing nothing but rolling on each other!" and they all started laughing.

Bruce said, "Fuck you!" The boys then all got to work.

That day when they were all hard at work, it was just like the gang had figured. Silk had bought Champ a brand-new pair of high top, black All-Stars and told him to put them on and give him his old ones. Then he said to Champ, "Now you look like one of my boys."

That day was pretty much the same as the last: wash, rinse, dry, and wax, repeatedly until something happened. A car pulled into the car wash. It was a Cadillac; the sharpest one that Champ had ever seen. It was two-toned emerald green with white leather exterior and a matching leather top, with gold grill bumpers, door handles, an emblem, gold Dayton wires with vogue tires, with a fifth wheel tagging behind. In those days for a Fleetwood Brougham to be like that, the owner wasn't working at a post office. He watched it as it coasted into the number five cover, and the driver hopped out of the car nice and easy.

He was a fella in his early thirties, well-groomed with a long jerry curl that ran past his shoulder, and a light mustache and beard. He closed the door and started walking toward Champ with a stride that evoked coolness, calmness, and confidence. He wore a pair of tailor-made slacks with a matching long-sleeved shirt that was tucked into his waistline, and a belt that matched his shoes like Champ's Pops wore. When he got to Champ, he said, "Just wipe it down, Lil' man."

Champ was still watching him as he walked by. He went to the bucket and got a wet towel, wrung it out then went over to the Cadillac. He started at the back and worked his way to the front. It was so clean that it probably wouldn't need a car wash for the next ten years. He had wiped the whole car, including the rims. The only thing left to do was the windows. So he went back over to his bucket, got his window cleaner, and went back to the car. He started on the windows, putting some water on the windshield and cleaning it. Then he moved on to the side windows, and that's when he saw her. She was the prettiest girl that Champ had ever seen, and she was sitting in the back seat of the Cadillac, watching him. She had sandy brown skin, hazel eyes, and three long plaits hanging down her back. They stared at each other for a few moments before a lady in the front seat turned around and said, "Sit your ass down and leave that damn boy alone!"

Champ started back cleaning the windows. When the guy came back to the car, he handed him ten dollars and said, "Alright Lil' man. Thanks."

He replied, "Anytime." He got into the Cadillac and pulled away.

The rest of the day all Champ could think about was that girl and he wished that he could see her again. Since there weren't any cars to be washed, Champ caught himself a nice shady spot under one of the covers and chilled until Silk came out of the office and looked around for the gang, only to see that everyone was busy except for him. He called Champ to come over to him. When he got there, he gave Champ a small paper bag and asked him if he had ever been in front of the fruit stand.

"Yep," Champ replied. He told him to take the bag to the Fruit Man. He told him to tell the Fruit Man that Silk said thanks.

Champ cuffed the bag under his arm and started toward the fruit stand, when Silk said, "Oh! And Champ?" He turned around to face him, "Don't forget the money."

Champ said, "Okay" and then continued on to the fruit stand. The man at the fruit stand gave him seventy dollars and two fresh peaches. He ate them on the way back to the car wash.

When Champ arrived, he gave the money to Silk. Silk said, "Alright Lil' man, good job."

That night after the car wash closed, Silk was sitting behind his desk in his office and the guy who was in the Cadillac sat across from him. On top of the desk was a stack of U.S. currency. Silk said to the guy, "You know, I heard that Truck pulled in another young gun?"

"Oh yeah?" commented the guy. "Well, he didn't mention it to me when I spoke to him." He tossed a stack of bills into a duffle bag, counting one hundred and sixty two thousand dollars in total. Then he looked over at Silk and asked, "Well, did Truck put him in Potted Land?"

"I don't think so," Silk replied. "I saw him hanging out on the hot spot with one of Birdie's boys from Pigeon Town. I don't know what they are up to, but Truck knows that the hot spot is neutral grounds," he continued. The guy looked at Silk strangely, as he rested back in his seat. He wasn't amused at all. "Maybe he was having himself a drink or something," Silk continued, and noticed that the guy didn't want to hear it or believe it. So he said, "Redd, just let it go. Just forget it."

Redd continued to stare at Silk before he said, "Yeah, yeah. Let's get through with this shit so that I can get outta here."

Finally, at a quarter to three in the morning, they had finished counting the money which added up to one hundred and seventy five thousand dollars. Then Redd left. Silk stayed at the car wash that night. Redd didn't go straight home after he left the car wash. Instead, he drove to Pigeon Town to see a fella by the name of Birdie. He figured that with the money Birdie had, he wouldn't be hanging out this late. So he passed on over by his house and when he got there, he knocked on the door and a nice-looking female answered it. "Oh! Hey Redd, how you doing?" she said.

Redd looked at the female angrily and replied, "Bitch! Get Birdie to the door before I shove my foot up yo ass!" and the girl didn't say another word. She turned around and went to call Birdie.

Birdie was the kind of guy who would party all day, every day. He kept two or three cheap whores at his house, and Silk would call him a fake-ass sugar daddy pimp who pushed blow for a living. When Birdie came to the door, he wore a long, burgundy silk robe, which he was closing as he approached the door.

"Yeah, what's up Redd? What brings you over to this area?" he asked.

"Look! You sugar-footed mutha fucka!" Redd yelled. "Is anything going on between you and Truck on neutral grounds?" he asked.

Redd took a step closer to Birdie, making sure he was in striking distance. Birdie's eyes widened as he stuttered, "N-N-No, Redd! I have nothin' going on with Truck!" he said.

Redd said, "What about this young gun Truck's got that's supposed to be holding the hot spot down?"

"It's some kid that flew in just last week from the Bay area. You got to believe me, man! I don't have shit to do with him!"

Redd stared at Birdie for a few moments. He knew that he didn't know anything about the kid because if he did he would have cracked under pressure. Before he left, he left Birdie with these words, "Don't end up like the last mark." And then he was gone.

After leaving Birdie's house, Redd thought he'd pass by the hot spot and peep things out. When he approached the hot spot, it was just as if Silk had said. There was one of Birdie's boys, along with the new kid, hanging out in front of the hot spot and pushing blow. One or two days could be explained, but a week left no excuse. Redd pulled his Cadillac to the curb in front of the bar and got out with a long-nosed .44 magnum pistol in his hand. The two boys watched Redd the whole time, but they didn't expect anything until he raised the gun and pointed it at Birdie's boy…and then it hit him. Redd asked, "Do you work for Birdie?"

The kid replied, "Yep!"

As he nodded his head up and down, Redd shot him and said, "Not anymore." He then grabbed the new kid by his neck and directed him towards the Cadillac. Blood had splattered all over the new kid's shirt because Birdie's boy had been right next to him when he was shot. He opened the trunk of the Cadillac and put the kid in it. He closed it up, got in the car, and peeled off.

The next day when the boys made it to the car wash, they knew immediately that something was definitely wrong. Big Bruce yelled out, "Damn! This mutha fuckas empty!" as they stopped in their tracks and stared at an empty lot.

Then Busty said, "Damn. Look at Silk's Eldorado!" which was parked halfway under the fourth cover. It was riddled with bullet holes, and the windows were busted out. The boys ran closer to get a better look at the car, and found that it was in very bad shape. There were holes in the doors big enough for a baseball to go through. The radio was shot and the interior was ruined. Then they heard Silk's voice coming from his office.

They all went to his office and stood in the doorway. They heard him telling someone on the phone, "After I hit the first one, three more came tearing at me!" Then he noticed his boys standing in the doorway and told the person on the phone, "Hold up a minute, will ya?"

He dug into his pocket, pulled out a one hundred dollar bill, and handed it to Big Bruce. He told them that they didn't have to work today, and said that he wanted all of them to get fresh haircuts. He told them to go by Big Charlie's, and that he would call him and have him waiting for them. Champ looked over at the trash can, where there was one of Silk's khaki tops stuffed in it. It was bloody, so he figured that's why he sat in his office wearing only his cotton tank top. He couldn't figure out where Silk had been hit, but he was certain that he had been.

They all headed over to Big Charlie's and got haircuts. Then they made their way to the clubhouse. On their way there, they stopped by Big Head Simon's. Big Head Simon was an old man whose wife, Ms. Corean, would treat the gang to a slice of apple pie from time to time. They both took a liking to the gang and nearly everyone who had been living in the neighborhood for the last twenty years spoke of the wildest experiences about Big Head Simon. They said that he was an old gangster who sold moonshine for a living, and carried a double barrel shotgun on the seat of his pickup. When the gang got to Big Head Simon's house, Ms. Corean was waiting for them on the front porch with a fresh baked apple pie in her hands, smiling at them. "I knew my boys were coming," she said.

"Hey! Ms. Corean!" they all shouted.

"Y'all just sit y'allses Lil' tails down and rest a little. Because y'all kids just run, run, run!" she ordered, but in a friendly manner. She looked at Champ and asked, "Well! Who is this?"

"That's Bo brother!" shouted Dusty. She cocked her eyes toward him and said, "What did I tell you about that?"

Dusty then put his hand over his mouth, and she looked at Champ. She asked, "Now, what is your name, Sweetheart?"

Champ looked up at her and replied, "Champ." She looked at him up and down and then said, "What a fine young man you is! I bet the girls just go crazy over you!" and the gang started laughing.

She then turned and yelled towards the house for her husband Simon, "Simon! Come out here and see Bo's brother!" as she handed all of them a piece of the warm, fresh apple pie.

Big Head Simon came out on the porch and looked at all of the boys. He asked Ms. Corean, "Who you talkin' 'bout is Bo's brother?" When he spotted Champ, he took a few steps back to look at him real good.

"Well, what do you think? Might be the next black attorney or doctor, huh?" she said.

Big Head Simon stared at Champ and replied, "Corean, I'ma tell you just what I told you about that fat knucklehead."

"Simon you don't say--" Ms. Corean tried to finish but Big Head Simon cut her off.

"Um," he mumbled. "I smell gangster all over him."

They all froze, because Simon nearly scared the life out of them. In fact, they didn't say a word for some time. After leaving Ms. Corean's house, the sun began to set. But it wasn't time for the boys to go inside. They all decided to go and play around with the girls until it was time to go in. All the girls hung around Minnie's house. There were always a lot of women hanging around there because her godmother Janice fixed hair, and she stayed with her. When they made it to Minnie's house, there was a gang of girls there. They waved and giggled at the boys, and then one of the girls asked, "Which one of you is Champ?"

Champ was always stuck in the back of the crowd so that no one could see him, but it was just his luck. The gang stood aside so that he could be seen and said, "That's him, there."

The girls all started blushing as Busty yelled to them, "One of y'all go up in there and call Kay for me."

One of the girls said to another, "Nonny, go inside and tell Kay that Champ is out here."

While she was going to get Kay, the gang all found a spot

on the porch and started talking to the girls. All of the gang talked to them except Big Bruce. None of the girls liked him because he was fat. So to pass the time, he would crack jokes about them constantly.

When the girl came back, she stepped out on the porch but there was nobody else with her. She said, "Say boy!" And Champ turned around to look at her, "My momma want you!"

He looked at Busty and Bo with his eyes wide, and they started chuckling. Big Bruce said, "Go in there, man. She ain't gon' do you nothing." Then the rest of the gang began to say things like:

"What you scared fo?"

"Go in and come right out!"

"That's your girlfriend."

"They just want to see how cute you are."

Then the girls said, "Come on, boy! We gon' bring you in there! Boy, don't be scared!" Then they all crowded around Champ and took him inside the house.

He could hear Dusty in the background teasingly, "Oh! He is so cute!"

When he got inside the house, there were a lot of women getting their hair fixed. Some were under the hair dryer, and others were getting their hair rolled or hot curled. One lady looked at Champ and said, "Oh Jane Lee! He's a cute Lil' boy. Look!"

And then another lady turned around, looked at him, and asked, "Do you like my baby?" Champ smiled and held his head down. She said, "Hold your head up and talk to me."

He held his held up and looked at her, trying not to smile. He just couldn't help it, and she started smiling back at him. One lady who was getting her hair rolled said, "Oh no, Jane Lee! He can't have my godchild!"

Then another lady asked, "Why he can't, Glo?"

She replied, "Cause that Lil' boy ain't nothing but a heartbreaker!"

Kay walked into the room and Champ knew that it was her right away, because he recognized the long plaits and the big titties. He thought she was so fine. The lady looked at Kay and asked her, "Now, who do you want calling here; him or Damien?"

Kay pointed at Champ, "Him."

The lady that went by the name of Glo said, "Well, that's good, because I didn't like that bad ass other Lil' boy anyway!"

Then her aunt looked at Champ and asked, "You gon' take care of my baby?" He nodded his head up and down, still smiling, and then she said, "He can't stop smiling, Glo. Look at him."

"I see him blushing," Glo replied.

That was pretty much it. They went back on the porch with the rest of the kids and Champ told them that they just loved him in there. Once they were on the porch, they started talking to each other. She said, "Boy! You know all the girls around here been talking about you?"

"What they been talking about me for?" he asked.

She smacked him on the shoulder softly and said, "Because they like you, Stupid."

Then one girl yelled out, "She always want to hit people." Kay looked at her and rolled her eyes.

Then Champ told her that he didn't like any of the girls. She started laughing and said, "They said you are cuter than Donkey!" They all thought that was funny, too.

Donkey knew that he had a lot of girlfriends so he just smacked his lips at the remark, but his girlfriend Bianca who lived across the street replied, "He don't look better than Donkey!" as she gave everyone a crazy look. But she liked Champ, too!

That night, it had gotten late. Champ wanted to get a goodnight kiss from Kay, but he was too shy to ask her for one before they all went home. After they got home and settled in, they found out that something terrible had happened because Ms. Katt yelled, "Bo! Champ! Y'all come here and hurry up!" Bo and Champ rushed out of the bedroom to the living room where Ms. Katt was watching the nightly news. They both sat on the couch next to her and she told them to watch.

It broadcast a gun battle in mid-city that had turned fatal. She explained to them that Silk had been shot, along with another accomplice, who had been killed. The news reporter said that one of the victims had been rushed to Charity Hospital where he was under guarded supervision, and that his condition was undetermined. Everyone in the neighborhood loved Silk, even Ms. Katt. Tears ran down her face as she whispered, "Hang in there, Silk. Everybody is praying for you." The boys started crying as well. Even though Champ hadn't known him very long, he still didn't want to see him go.

Since Silk had been shot, the car wash stayed closed for over a week. As the boys walked through it, everything seemed strange. Nothing was right since he was away. Even the fruit stand was closed, and the barber shop, too. Busty said that they were probably trying to raise money to bury Silk whenever he died. Dusty asked him why he always thought like that.

He replied, "Silk told me to think of the worst things that could happen."

It was a Saturday morning; two weeks after Silk had been shot. Bo and Champ woke up early to watch the Saturday morning cartoons. Ms. Katt would get her rest on Saturday's so instead of a hot breakfast they ate cereal. At around nine o'clock, there was a knock on the front door, and the boys ran to the front window to peep out. They saw the front end of Redd's Fleetwood Brougham, and that's when Bo went to the door and asked, "Who is it?"

"Sunshine," a lady replied.

"Hold up, I gotta call my Momma!" Bo replied, and ran into Ms. Katt's room to wake her.

She came to the door and opened it, saying, "Oh hey, Shiney!"

"Katt girl, I am sorry for waking you up early, but Silk sent me to get your boys."

Bo and Champ looked at each other, astounded. "Oh! Silk made it?" asked Ms. Katt.

"Yeah, girl," Shiney replied. "But he ain't gonna be able to walk no more, long as he living."

Ms. Katt then turned and told them to go and put some clothes on because she was going to let them go and see Silk. They got dressed and rushed out of the house with Sunshine. She had packed the whole gang into Redd's slick, green Fleetwood.

Sunshine was Redd's girl, the same lady who had been sitting in the front seat of the Cadillac that day at the car wash. She looked real good, in fact, and Champ stared at her the whole time from the house to the hospital. When they made it to the hospital she said, "Silky gon' be so glad to see y'all!"

It wasn't hard for them to find Silk; his room number was 916. When they entered the room, Dusty was amazed at all of the balloons that surrounded Silky's bed and door. They all followed behind Sunshine as she opened the door and said, "Here they go, Silk."

The gang walked into the room and Silk was sitting up in his bed, talking to Redd. He looked at them and smiled as they entered. Both sides of the bed were lined with balloons and flowers, which read "Get Well Soon." They all ran to his bedside and Busty nearly cried, "Silk, we thought you was gon' die!"

He rubbed him on his head and replied, "Nah, Busty. Silk is a soldier!"

Big Bruce replied, "That's what I want to be!"

Redd asked, "So you want to be a soldier, boy?" He looked at Bruce while rubbing his goatee.

"Yep!" Big Bruce replied. "Just like Silk!"

Dusty shouted, "But Silk, you told me you was a G!"

Silk and Redd looked at each other and smiled. Silk said, "Come here, Lil' Dee." That's what he called him at work, and as Dusty came closer to his bed the whole room became silent. Silk looked at him and said, "Lil' Dee, you right 'bout that. I did tell you that I'm a G." And then he looked around at the rest of the gang, "But I am a soldier in combat." Then he raised his hand up to point at the boys, "And right now, y'all are too young to be G's."

That's when Redd spoke out and said, "Y'all soldiers." All the boys felt proud.

Big Bruce whispered to himself, "Soldier boys."

Silk had been in the hospital for nearly a month before the doctor allowed him to come home. He stayed home for a few days before he went back to the car wash. The car wash hadn't been open in nearly a month. So when it did reopen, there were cars parked everywhere. It seemed as if everyone who would usually bring his or her car over on a certain day was there on the day that Silk came home. It was like a big celebration. There was a barbecue grill set up outside the office with chips, sodas, and hot dogs. While the boys washed cars, Silk and Redd sat outside of the office greeting everyone who came. It seemed as if everyone that came had something for Silk. All the guys in silk shirts and pretty cars gave him money. All the women gave him flowers or a gift.

Champ had just finished drying a long, white Buick Riviera and had started on the tires with some Armor All when Redd's pretty green Cadillac showed up. It was his girl Sunshine, and that pretty girl who was in the back seat. There was no room for the Cadillac on the lot, so she parked it a distance down the middle of the block. Sunshine and the girl came walking into the car wash parking lot just moments later. Champ couldn't keep his eyes off her. She wore a sleeveless sundress with flowers on it, a pair of brown sandals, and she had those long plaits. She never noticed him watching her from the other side of the lot, and as much as he wanted to walk over and ask her name, he didn't. Champ didn't know the first thing to say to her so he just continued to stare at her. He figured that she'd be hanging around for the most of the day, so he thought that he would have plenty of time to talk to her.

Champ had finished the tires on the Riviera and was preparing to move on to the next car, which was a brown Cadillac Seville. He sat his bucket down and opened the door to do the inside because Silk had told him to always start on the inside of the car. He pulled the floor mats out of the car, and then used his small broom to sweep the floor of the car. All of a sudden, someone asked, "What is your name?"

From the sound of that voice, Champ knew that it couldn't be anyone but her. So he turned around to look at her and she stood there with her arms folded across her chest. He asked her to repeat what she had asked. "I asked your name," she replied.

He stood in front of her and said, "My name is Champ. What is yours?"

"Sand" she replied, and then looked over toward the office where Silk and Redd were having a few laughs. Then she looked back at Champ.

"Silk your daddy, huh?" he asked.

She looked Champ in his eyes for a few seconds and then started laughing. With the broom still in his hand, he looked at her with a curious expression. He asked, "What's funny?"

She looked him up and down and then asked, "You don't have a girlfriend, huh?"

Champ was speechless, because then he thought about Kay. She was his girlfriend, but he wanted Sand to be his girlfriend, too. So he made a serious face and replied, "I got a lot of girlfriends," and hoped it worked.

She yelled out playfully, "You lying your ass off!"

"Girl, I do!" he said. Then she told him to name one, and he began to stutter.

She replied, "Uh-huh. Look at you there. You can't even name one."

He just stared at her and tried to hold his smile back as much as possible. Then she asked him if he cared for a chili dog because she was headed to get one. He knew that she would be his. He said he would like one, and she turned around and started toward the food table to get the food. He finished the Seville before she returned. When she returned with the chilidogs and handed one to him, she said, "I don't know why you are so shy, because I know a lot of boys who don't have girlfriends." Champ bit down on the chilidog and looked at her. Then she asked, "Do you have a phone?"

"Why? You want my number?" he asked.

Then she looked over at her Daddy, then back at Champ and said, "Because I'ma call you, Stupid!"

Then he asked her, "Are you going to be my girlfriend?"

She replied quickly, "Yep!" And he smiled.

Later on that day, Silk sat behind his desk in his wheelchair and the boys all copped a spot inside his office. Everyone had left, so they shut the car wash down and gathered in his office to find out what was so important that Silk needed to talk to them about. When they were all settled down in the office, he said, "I just want to tell y'all that, um…a lot of things is not going to be the same. Old Silk here been forced to sit down now." He looked down at his wheelchair. "I know that I been asking y'all to run a few errands for me here and there, and that y'all don't want to do it sometimes." They all attempted to say something. "Hold up!" Silk said. "Just listen to me," and he took a deep breath. "You see, it is going to be kind of hard for old Silk to do a lot of things," he said as he looked at all of the kids. "Things like go to the grocery store, payin' my bills, makin' sure my people get took care of, iron my clothes. And boys, the list goes on and on."

Silk opened his arms wide, and slowly he said, "Y'all got old Silk. Yeah, I got money, nice clothes, fly cars, 'n whores." He dropped his hands to his side and said, "But I ain't never had a family." When he said that, tears flooded the wells of all of their eyes. "There was never any love in it for me," he continued. "I didn't have anybody to tell me not to do this, and not to do that. Nobody to trust. I ain't had nobody to run to when I had a problem. New Year's to New Year's Eve, it was all about a dollar. That's why I want y'all to remember that even though the record broke, it never rained on Silk's party." Silk meant every word he said. They realized right then how much they meant to him and how much he meant to all of them, too.

Big Bruce stood up and walked over to Silk's wheelchair and said, "We'll be your family, Silk."

Silk looked around and said, "It's a long way to the hilltop. Y'all think y'all ready?"

The boys all nodded their heads and Busty said, "We soldiers, remember?"

Silk laughed and replied, "Yeah! Lil' man, I remember." They smiled, and that's when Silk said, "Oh yeah! And another thing I want to tell y'all. Save yo' money, because whenever yo' Lil' girlfriends ask to go to the show or the arcade you will have some money to take her and treat her nice." Then he looked at Champ and said, "Champ, I saw you over there putting your mack down on Redd's daughter, Sand," and the gang started laughing. Champ just smiled.

Then Dusty teased and cried out, "Oh, he is sooo cute."

Silk looked at Champ with a sneaky grin and said, "Champ, you ain't nothing but Silky Slim in his prime." He rubbed his goatee and mumbled.

That night, Silk paid them and they all went home. For some strange reason, Champ found himself thinking about what Silk had told them about the 'broken record at the party.' He had to look at the television for a while to try and get it off of his mind, even though he hadn't the slightest idea what Silk had been talking about. Hell, he didn't recall anything going wrong with the music at the car wash.

CHAPTER THREE

5 Years later (July 1986)

Champ had just made his fifteenth birthday, and a lot of things had changed in the past five years. Big Bruce and Dusty had moved in with Silk right after he got shot. Actually, Silk never went anywhere without Bruce on his side. When they all made thirteen, Silk taught them how to drive, except for Dusty because he was still too young. A lot of people used to stare at Silk when they saw Bruce driving him around in his Cadillac.

Donkey's girl Bianca slipped and got pregnant at fifteen, and everybody in the neighborhood was talking about it. She had a baby boy on Silk's birthday. Bianca wanted to name the baby William, but after it was all said and done, Donkey persuaded her to name the baby Herman. Donkey had a cousin named Herman, or Herm for short, from Back-A-Town.

Herm would come around every now and then and chill, and yes, he was cool. The first time they all started smoking pot was with him. Ever since then, the gang would sit under the fifth cover whenever there was nothing to do and get high. Everybody had a certain thing they would do when they got high, besides laughing a lot. Bruce would go eat, and Dusty would tag along with him. Nobody could split them up. Busty wouldn't do or say anything when he was high. It's as if he would turn into a mummy or something. He would just watch everyone. As for Champ, Donkey, and Bo, they would play with the girls.

Donkey and Bianca would always argue if she had an idea that he was messing with another girl. Bo and Minnie would always be on bad terms. They were together for a while and then they wouldn't be speaking, and then they would get back together again. As for Champ, he didn't know who he liked the most, Sand or Kay. Silk would always ask him if he had chosen yet. He knew that he wanted them both. He thought it was love that he felt for them, but he never told them. Champ just kept that a secret. The gang thought he had got in them draws. When they asked he would just say, "Man, I don't kiss and tell."

There were some changes in his real family, too. After eleven years, Champ's momma had found out about Ms. Katt. Pops wasn't around to see the sparks fly, though. He was caught by the police with some drugs and sent to prison. There was a big conflict between the two women. It was always about who was going to see him. So, he didn't allow either one of them to come.

Bo and Champ would ride up to the penitentiary with Pop's best friend Leroy, once a month. Leroy kept his El Dog in the garage at his mother's house. Pops said that if Champ graduated from high school, he could take the El Dog to the prom. His stepsister, Holly, had a baby from a fella named Reuben. He was now in jail for murder, but since he was only an accomplice to the murder, the judge sentenced him to seven years in the state penitentiary. Pops told Champ that the pen was so big that it would probably be seven years before he probably would ever see him. Since Holly had a baby, that made her eligible for an apartment and welfare, so she got one in the Magnolia Projects. The whole gang would sleep over there most of the time. Her house was like their clubhouse.

One day they all went to a game room where all the older kids hung out. They usually shot pool, played games, or just hung around. Whenever Silk saw them, there he would tell them to stay away from it because it was not a place for them to be, but they ignored him most of the time.

One day some trouble started between Donkey and this fella from the projects named Wendell. Most of the guys who lived there were jealous of Donkey ever since elementary school. Donkey and Champ were shooting a game of pool when he made a mistake and hit Wendell with the butt of the pool stick. He said, "Excuse me," but Wendell didn't want to hear it.

Wendell started shoving Donkey around and saying, "Mutha fucka, you don't know me!" He continued to shove and curse Donkey. It took a lot to upset Donkey, because he was more of a player than a gangster. Champ knew that he didn't want to fight Wendell, even though he was pushing him.

Champ stepped between the both of them and said to Wendell,
"Say, Bro! He don't want to fight you!"

Wendell looked at Champ with a frown and said, "Get the fuck out of my way!" as he shoved Champ into the jukebox.

Bo struck him in the face and yelled, "Bitch! Don't hit my brother!" He and Bo started fighting and then they all started ganging him. He fell to the floor and they kicked, stomped, and punched him until blood started splashing everywhere. All of a sudden, they heard a bottle bust but didn't pay any attention to it because they all were still focused on Wendell. Donkey returned to the squabble and started stabbing Wendell with the broken bottle. Everyone froze and watched him stab Wendell repeatedly. They were all shocked, because they had never seen him like this before. He finally stopped stabbing him, stood over his body with the bottle dripping with blood, and yelled, "Bitch! You don't know me!"

When the fight first started, the handful of people that were in the game room ran out. The only person that was still in there was the owner, named Mr. Scott. He yelled for them to stay right where they were because he was calling the police. Busty grabbed Donkey by his arm and yelled, "Come on man! Let's go!" They all ran out of the game room.

So there they went, high tailing it down the street like five bats out of hell. Donkey had so much of Wendell's blood all over his clothes that they thought that he was the one bleeding. They got just blocks from the carwash on Rocheblave Street and stopped. The boys were scared and tired, and didn't know what to do at first. Finally, Bo asked, "Donkey, you didn't kill him, did ya?"

Busty mumbled, "Man. Wendell will never get well."

Dusty added to it by saying, "You mean he gon' die?" and then he went into a panic and started crying.

"Shut up, Dusty!" Busty yelled as he snatched him by his shirt collar and instructed him to pull himself together. Then he looked at the rest of them and said that they had to hide Donkey. The whole time Donkey stood silently with his bloody hands in his pockets, and they knew that he was scared, too.

Then Bo said, "We can send Dusty to get Bruce. He will know what to do!" All of them looked to Bruce because they knew that he was always right. Dusty ran to get Bruce.

"Come on, man! Get in!" Bruce yelled as he pulled up in Silk's Fleetwood with Dusty on the passenger side. After explaining to Bruce what had happened, the first thing he said they had to do was to get Donkey somewhere safe. So they all headed to Holly's house. When they got there, Busty said, "Man, we can't just sit around, bro!"

"We gotta find something to do, and quick!" shouted Bo, as they all sat around scared as hell.

Champ looked at the gang and said, "Whatever we do, we can't let Silk find out!"

"I'm telling ya!" yelled Dusty as he held his head down.

Then he mumbled, "Man, we should've stayed away from the game room like he said."

Bruce walked into the room with a handful of cookies and said, "I know what we can do." He bit into one of the cookies.

Champ said, "What?" They were all ears for ideas.

Bruce flopped down on the bed and said, "Tomorrow night we can go over to Mr. Scott's game room just before it closes," and he looked around at all of us as he continued, "Then when he leave, we can put a bullet in his ass."

Then the whole gang yelled at the same time, "Man! We ain't killing anybody else!"

"Where did you get that from?" asked Dusty, as the boys stared at him angrily.

Bruce shrugged his shoulder while biting down on a cookie and replied, "That's how Silk n' em do it."

"What is you talking about?" asked Bo.

Busty quickly interrupted, "He's right!" Then everybody looked at him as he continued, "I heard Silk say something about if there's no witnesses, there's no case."

"So what does that mean?" Donkey asked.

Busty replied, "Mr. Scott is the only person who saw you kill Wendell, so he is a witness."

"Then the witness got to go." Bruce replied. He added, "Or you can go to the pen!"

Everybody was silent for a moment and stared at Donkey, as he held his head down in despair. Then he raised his head up and stated, "Tomorrow night. Mr. Scott got to go."

So, it was final. They were going to kill Mr. Scott tomorrow night in order to keep Donkey from going to the pen. But they needed a gun to do it. Donkey called his cousin, Herm, and had him bring them a pistol. Later that night, Herm brought them a .38 special that would shoot five times. However to be on the safe side, Champ also took his mom's old .22 long-nose from off the top shelf in the hallway closet. That made it eight shots which could come in handy.

That night, everybody went inside early and was too scared to say a word. They knew what they had to do, and they knew that it was a must to get it done. They all had thoughts about what would happen if any of them got caught, but it was a chance that they all had to take. The next morning came and nobody went to work at the car wash. The gang was sure that the bad news had spread around the neighborhood and they were right about that.

The news did spread fast, too fast, because the police kicked down Holly's door at a quarter to eight that morning. They had a search warrant for one Derrick Louis AKA Donkey. The police handcuffed him and put him in the back seat of the police car. They took him down town to the Juvenile Bureau where he was booked for first-degree murder. Their world caved in, and then they were really forced to do what they didn't want to do...that was, commit another murder.

"I told y'all time and time again, not to hang around that game room!" shouted Silk, as the boys sat in his office with their heads down because they knew they had disobeyed him. He sat in his wheelchair, angry as hell. After about a half hour of fussing at them, he rested back in his chair and just stared at them. They couldn't look him in his eyes because they all knew that they had goofed up.

He began speaking again, saying, "I told y'all a long time ago when I was coming up, the train that I rode on never came through. But I still made it!" As he expressed himself with hand motions, he continued, "But y'all don't want to listen! And it's only a few things that I can help you with now." Then he turned his wheelchair around to face the back of them and said, "As for this one, I can't help you at all."

Tears started to flood the wells of the boys' eyes, because of Silk turning his back on them. That was like someone putting a gun to their heads and squeezing the trigger. Everything was hush-hush in the office. Donkey was in jail; Silk turned his back on them; what was next? They had lost all hope. There was nothing else for them to do. As the tears ran down their faces, Champ stood up and said, "Remember what you said about the broken record?" He knew that Silk was listening to him because his muscles flinched. So he continued, "It never rained on your party then."

Everybody stayed quiet, even Champ. Then Silk turned around to face him, looking him directly in his eyes and said, "There is only one way it won't rain on this party, Champ, but I will have nothing to do with it." Bruce was right. Silk said exactly what Bruce said he would. "Get rid of the witnesses." But he also said that they would have to do it at their own risk, which meant that he wasn't giving them any guns or anything. His only advice was, "Handle your business." Worse, they had to do it without Donkey because he was still in jail.

There were only two guns, so only two of them were going. Just before the sun went down, they had an unexpected guest. It was Donkey's cousin, Herm, who showed up at Holly's house in a stolen car. He had a gun. He said that Donkey let him know what was up. He told Champ to come along to make sure everything went fine.

The game room closed at ten o'clock. It was a quarter after nine, and they were still at Holly's house talking. Herman asked, "Have any of you ever killed anyone?" and they all shook their heads to indicate that they hadn't. Then they asked Herm if he had ever killed anyone before, and he leaned back on the sofa and replied, "Yeah. I killed a man before. Popped a few. But I don't feel good about it too much," he said.

Bruce asked, "Why not?"

Herm looked at him and replied, "I can't explain it to ya' because I don't understand it myself. Maybe I'm too young to understand. All I can tell you is, that shit is fucked up."

At about a quarter to ten, Champ, Busty, and Herm headed to the game room. Bruce wanted to come along, and even though Herman said that four would be too many, he still came along, just to be on the safe side. At five minutes to ten, the game room was empty. Mr. Scott would usually be cleaning up by then. Herm parked the car on the corner from the game room and said that he was going in to ask for some change. He said that if he didn't come out in three minutes for the rest of them to come in, because that would mean that nobody was in there but him. They all agreed, so he got out of the car and headed toward the game room. Champ was shaking like a leaf on a tree, and had butterflies in his stomach. After three minutes was up they tied bandanas around their faces, hopped out of the car and headed into the game room.

"Bitch! This is a robbery!" Busty yelled as he pointed the .38 in Mr. Scott's face. Herm pulled out his gun, walked back to the front door, and closed it.

Champ grabbed Mr. Scott by his shirt collar and dragged him to the center of the floor, as he begged for his life. "Please, don't kill me! Please!"

As Champ instructed him to get on his knees, Busty was getting the money out of the register and Herm yelled, "Man, just kill this nigga and let's go!" Champ looked at Busty, nodded his head toward the door, and then everything happened so fast.

Busty started toward the door and Champ took two steps back from Mr. Scott, who was still on his knees, yelling "No! Please don't!" and that's when Champ pulled the trigger once, and then again. Mr. Scott fell onto his back with five bullets in his chest. There wasn't much blood. Champ took one more look at the body, and then bolted toward the door.

All of a sudden, Herm said, "Hold up. Don't leave yet!" He turned and walked over to Mr. Scott's body, pointed his gun, and shot him four more times. This time it was in his head. Then there was a great deal of blood, and it splattered everywhere. They all ran out of the game room, got in the car, and left quickly.

After they killed Mr. Scott, Herm dropped them all off at Holly's house and he left. Later on, they found out he went to jail that night for the stolen car. They never learned what happened to the gun, though.

That night, Donkey made a phone call to Holly's house from the Juvenile Bureau saying that he didn't like it in there, and that he thought some guys was going to gang up on him. They told him what happened, and that it wouldn't be long before he came home. The next day, they all went to work and Silk called them in the office so that he could have a talk with them. When they were settled in his office he said, "I saw the news this morning and it seems as if old Scottie had an accident," and he looked around at all of the boys. Then he continued, "I don't want to know who did it, but I like the way that business was taken care of."

Then he told Bruce to get him a soda from the icebox in the back room. "So I'ma tell you like this boys; y'all growing up now, and y'all have a choice. Either y'all hang around here and wash cars for the next ten years, or y'all can advance," he said as he popped the cap on the soda. "But that I'ma leave up to y'all," and he raised the soda up to his lips and took a swallow. Then he looked around at all of them and said, "One simple answer." They all looked at each other because they didn't know what to say.

Silk got angry and shouted, "Simple, damn it! You wash cars, or you get paid!" Everybody stood silent. They were puzzled. Silk sat impatiently and waited for an answer. He sat staring at each and every one of them. He was looking into their eyes as if trying to look into each of their souls, because he was drawing the line and wanted to know on which side of it they stood. He saw that there wasn't going to be an answer and said, "Well alright then, y'all go ahead and get your things ready. The cars should be pulling up in about a minute."

"I'm in!" Big Bruce shouted abruptly.

Silk looked astonished. Then Bo stood up and said, "Me, too!" That's when all the boys stood up.

Silk looked around at them and said, "Then I think I better tell y'all what I do for a living." He opened up his desk drawer. He reached in for something and then tossed it on the desktop. It was a clear plastic bag with a bunch of small red balls inside of it. The boys all looked as he took one of the balls from the bag and sat it on the desk. He said, "This is a dose of heroin and it cost thirty five dollars a dose. It'll be bagged like this." He picked up the bag and continued by saying, "I'ma give y'all bags that will have forty doses in it and a whole bag is worth fourteen hundred dollars. You are to take no shorts under any circumstances."

Then he looked at each and every one of them to make sure that they all understood. He then picked up a ball and said, "For every dose sold I get twenty and y'all get fifteen. Is that understood?" The boys nodded their heads. He told them to help him to the car because they were going shopping with him. Silk took them to Canal Street to shop. School was about to start in a couple of months and he wanted the gang to look nice, because they were his boys, AKA Soldier Boys. He took them to a store called Ruberstein Brothers, and then to another one called Nowaks. They each picked up a few pair of Hushpuppies shoes that Silk said the girls liked, and some snakeskin belts, too. All of their eyes were on the large selection of silk shirts at Nowaks, but the boys picked up a few other shirts called Holy Casino. After buying some pants to match the shirts, they were all set for the first day of school.

Donkey stayed in the Juvenile Detention Center for about a month before the judge released him. He had to let him go because they didn't have a case. The judge told him that if he ever came before him again, that he would send him to Scotlandville for a long time. Everyone knew it was where juveniles served long terms. Donkey came home a week before school started, so Silk took him shopping for some school clothes as well. They filled him in on everything that was going on.

Silk insisted that the boys save their money so they put everything they made into a wooden box in Holly's hallway closet. They had only saved about two grand, but they were all still hustling and soon all that changed a lot. For every bundle that they sold, they made six hundred dollars. They would sell at least thirteen bundles a day. It seemed as if every day the business got better and better. Redd would drop off a package at the car wash every week. Every week before Silk scored, he would have them all in his office counting the stacks of money. By the time school started, the gang had saved up forty three thousand dollars, and it was steadily increasing.

The first day of school came and the boys were all ready. Everybody went to a high school called Walter L. Cohen, except for Dusty who was too young. Therefore, he went to a school closer to Holly's house called Carter G. Woodson.

When the gang arrived in front of the school everybody was staring at them as they hopped out of Silk's big Fleetwood Brougham. They had to be the cleanest gang of guys there that year. Champ had on a long-sleeved, Navy blue shirt with a pair of denim Levi's, a snakeskin belt, and a pair of plush navy blue suede low-top Hushpuppies. Busty wore a pair of dark brown Levi's with a beige Holy Casino shirt, a Gator silk belt, and a pair of beige suede Hushpuppies. Bo wore a pair of black Levi's, a gray silk shirt, a pair of gray Hushpuppies, and a gatorskin belt. Donkey wore a pair of denim Levi's, a burgundy and white striped Holy Casino shirt, a snakeskin belt, and a pair of burgundy Hushpuppies. But all eyes were on Big Bruce. He really turned a lot of heads when he stepped out. He wore a dark green, long-sleeved silk shirt with a pair of white Levi's, a pair of green Hushpuppies with white leather hand pouches hanging from his wrist, a gold chain with a sacred cross on it, and a dark green Kangol cap tilted to the side. Silk sat in his car and watched his boys walk into the schoolyard. He just smiled.

Everybody in school had heard about Mr. Scott getting killed and everybody wanted to be their friends. Champ couldn't talk to too many girls, because he had to watch out for Sand; she was watching him like a hawk. A girl couldn't even look at Champ without her getting mad. In his first period class, Champ was the center of attention. The teacher, Ms. Watkins, was an attractive young woman of about 28 or so. She was fine. When the bell rang and all the students were settled in, she turned and wrote her name on the board. It was Donkey, Sand, and Champ, all in the same class. Champ sat behind Donkey and to Sand's left side, which was the last seat on the third row.

Ms. Watkins called the row to see if she saw any new faces that hadn't attended Cohen last year. Champ had gone to a school called Alcee Fortier the previous year, so he knew that he was one of the new faces she was looking for. When she called the name Wayne Randolph, Champ raised his hand and responded, "Right here!"

All of the class turned and looked over at him. Ms.

Watkins asked, "What school did you transfer from, Wayne?"

Champ replied, "Fortier."

She made a notation in her notebook and then said, "Okay" and moved on.

Bruce, Bo, Busty, Donkey's girl Bianca, Bo's girl Minnie, and a gang of old friends were all together in a different class. That class was buck wild! There were airplanes flying around the room, and paper balls getting thrown at the teacher. Somebody erased Ms. from in front of Ms. Jones' name and put "Mr." in its place. Big Bruce had all the fellas gathered in a circle, cracking jokes. While Busty had all the girls gathered around him talking "player shit" as he called it, Bo and Minnie sat in the back, hugging and kissing. Yes, Ms. Jones' class was out of control.

At lunch, they all sat at the table with the most girls and munched down. Everywhere Champ went, his girl Sand was sure to be there. She was just letting it be known to the other girls that they had something going on between them. Champ was so glad that Kay didn't go to the same school, because then it would be a big conflict between them. Kay was a senior at a private school called Xavier Prep, which was a school for girls. Her parents had a lot of money and they insisted that she attend the best schools. Although she went to a different school, Champ still had to watch himself whenever he was with Sand. Kay's stepsister Minnie was hanging around all the time, trying to keep her eyes on Bo.

After school was over, they all walked to the Louisiana bus stop to catch the bus home. What did Champ think of his first day of school? Well, he felt more like a senior than a sophomore. To be honest, he got more attention than the star point guard did on the basketball team and the star quarterback of the football team. On the bus as they were heading home, the boys were shooting the breeze with a guy named Ronnie who went to school with Dusty in elementary. He asked them if they were going to the Back-to-School Jam that one of the students was giving at the I.L.A. Hall. Bruce looked at the gang with a sneaky grin on his face. They had never been to anything like that. Hell, Champ was still a virgin at fifteen. They looked at each other. Sand spoke and said, "Yeah! Y'all going to the jam? Because we gon' go!"

"Yep, cuz, it's going to be nice!" shouted Minnie.

And that's when Big Bruce said, "Yeah, Bro, we going to the jam."

When they got off at the bus stop, everybody went to the car wash. Champ started walking Sand to her house. While they were walking along with the rest of the girls, he noticed Minnie peeping at them every now and then. She walked ahead with the rest of the girls. Champ couldn't do anything about it. He knew that she was sure to tell her sister about how he was acting around Sand. He was thinking that whatever was going to happen would happen. While they were walking, Sand asked Champ, "Why do you be smiling and shit?" He looked at her with a curious look on his face. "Don't look stupid, Champ," she continued, "Cause you know what I am talking about."

He asked, "What?"

"When them hoes be looking in your face, you just be smiling your ass off."

"Them hoes be smiling at me?" He tried to play dumb.

She jerked her hand away from him and said, "Yeah! And you be liking it, too!" He started smiling again. "It's funny huh?" she asked sarcastically.

Champ asked her if she was jealous and she just smacked her lips. He knew that she was mad at him because the girls at school were telling her that he looked good. Champ snatched her by her arms and pulled her body close to his, and gave her a long, warm, passionate kiss. She relaxed her body in his arms, as he slowly lowered his hand down to rest on her ass. Then they heard somebody yell, "Get! Get from in front of my house with that!" An old lady ran out her front door with a broom in her hand. They both started laughing as they ran up the street to catch up with the other girls. The old lady mumbled as they left, "That's what wrong with y'all kids now. Babies having babies."

Champ walked Sand to her friend Bianca's house where she would wait until her momma came to pick her up. He told her that he would see her tonight at the jam. She replied "Yeah! I'ma make sure that I'm there so I can keep an eye on your playboy ass," and then she smiled at him. He followed Bianca into her house. As he turned to walk downstairs, he saw Minnie standing in the doorway of her house. She had been watching them the whole time. Little did he know that Sand was peeping out of her window, too.

Champ continued down the stairs and went to the car wash. When he got to the car wash, he walked right into an argument between Donkey and this dope fiend named Quarter Horse. They called him that because he had a scooped up a Buick Deuce and a Quarter that ran like a racehorse. The argument was over Donkey not taking sixty-five dollars from him for two balloons. "Nigga, go head on and take this nickel short from old horse. You know I'm coming back."

Quarter Horse yelled and Donkey shouted back at him, "Mutha fucka! I don't take no shorts!" and then dropped the sixty-five dollars on the ground. Donkey continued, "Now you better be on your way fo' shit turn out bad!"

Quarter looked down at his money on the ground, then back at Donkey, and said, "Pick it up" in a low, evil tone.

"I ain't picking up shit!" said Donkey.

Then Quarter came closer to Donkey and said, "You see, you don't have no respect."

Champ knew he was trying to get a clear shot at Donkey, so he walked in between the two of them and picked up the money. He handed it to Quarter Horse and said, "I'm sorry Horse, but we don't take no shorts."

When he attempted to say, "But I, Quarter Hor---," Champ interrupted abruptly.

"Under no circumstances!" Champ shouted to him.

Just then they heard Silk's voice from the office, "The boy said he don't take no shorts, Quarter!" There ain't no telling how long he had been sitting there. Quarter Horse looked at Silk, then at Donkey, and snatched his money from Champ's hand.

"That's why I hate you pretty mutha fuckas!" shouted Quarter. Then he walked to his car and left.

After he left, Silk called them into his office and told Donkey, "You know he ain't coming back, right?"

Donkey nodded his head, looked around and said, "But Silk, I tri-"

"*Chill out!*" Silk yelled, cutting off Donkey. "I understand you had to do what you had to do," he continued as he turned his wheelchair around to go back into his office. Then he said, "Now y'all two come here. I want to show you something." They followed him into the office. Silk rolled his wheelchair behind his desk and opened up the desk drawer. Then reached in it and pulled out a gun. It was a large one. He placed the gun on his desk. He said, "Now tell me something," as he stared at them. "Do y'all know how to handle these?" They both looked at him and nodded their heads up and down. "Oh, yeah?" he asked, and rested back in his wheelchair. "Then show me how to handle it." He slid the gun closer to the boys.

Donkey and Champ looked at each other, and Donkey hunched his shoulder. Champ picked it up, Silk quickly yelled, "Give me that damn gun!" and he snatched it from their hands.

"How do you know how to handle a gun, and you don't even know how to pick it up?" he asked. Silk placed the gun back on the desk then picked it up by its handle and said, "You pick up a gun like this." As they looked on, he pointed at a button on the side of the gun and said, "This is your safety button." He clicked it back and forth while saying, "On; Off. On; Off."

While hitting a button he said, "This is your release button," and something dropped from the handle. He said that it was called a clip and even sometimes a magazine, and this is where the bullets went. He slipped it back into the handle of the gun and then said, "This is a Colt 45" as he rotated it around in his hand. "It is also known as an Army 45, because it was mostly used in the military. It carries eight bullets in the clip and one in the chamber. Now come here! Let me show you how to hold a gun."

It went on and on, and they did everything that they could do with a gun, except shoot it. He promised to take them to the shooting range one day to practice on their shots. After dealing with the gun for about an hour and a half, he said, "Now y'all listen to me," as he placed the gun back in the drawer. "In this game, don't nobody love you, but you." He looked the both of them in their eyes, "Because it ain't no love in this game. So you keep your friends close and your enemies closer. Y'all got that?" They both nodded.

Then he looked at Donkey and said, "And you! I want you to learn how to control your temper because they got people who won't be so calm, like Quarter Horse. So you work on that, okay?"

Donkey replied, "Alright."

Silk looked at him for a few seconds and then said, "Oh, yeah. I want you to straighten everything out between you and Quarter Horse, too." Donkey looked at Silk with a curious expression. Silk said, "Donkey, he could be a friend or an enemy; it doesn't matter, but you want him to be close by on any count. Now promise me whenever you get a chance that you'll do that for me?"

Donkey waited a second before he answered, then said, "Alright Silk, I'ma take care of that."

After the day was over and night fell, they were all at Holly's house getting dressed for the jam; everybody except Big Bruce. He was at the car wash trying to convince Silk that his car would be okay if he let them use it to go to the jam. "No way, Bruce!" shouted Silk. "You know I ain't gonna let you take my Cadi to no nighttime gig for youngsters!"

Big Bruce looked at Silk with a sorry expression and said, "Man, we ain't never been to no real jam like this, Silk. We just want to go and put our mack down on the women."

"I said no, Bruce!" yelled Silk. "And that is final!" Then he turned to watch the large color television that sat in his office.

Big Bruce couldn't believe that Silk wouldn't lend him the Cadi on an occasion like this. For a minute or two, he just stood there, stared at Silk, and finally said, "Alright Silk, I understand." Big Bruce walked out the door and started toward Holly's house. When Big Bruce left the office, Silk never noticed that he was gone until he turned around and said, "Bruce, get me a soda, will ya'?"

When he noticed that Bruce was gone, Silk yelled, "Ain't this some shit! The Lil' mutha fucka ain't even told me that he was leaving!" He started rolling his chair to the back of the office to get a soda. He began humming a Marvin Gaye tune to himself as he headed to the icebox. As Silk opened the fridge, a soda fell from the top shelf to the floor and burst open, splashing all over him. He yelled, "Bruce!"

After Big Bruce had left the office, Silk started feeling guilty about not lending him the Cadi, especially after all the things that he did for him. Out of the whole gang, Big Bruce was the one that he liked the most.

A bit later, even though Big Bruce was feeling down about not getting the Fleetwood, he was still going to go to the jam and have a good time. He mumbled to himself, *Even though the record broke, it never rained on Silk's party.* Suddenly, a car pulled up alongside of him and slammed on its brakes. Big Bruce froze up as he turned slowly to look at the car. When he saw the car and the driver, a smile came on his face big enough to tie a bow at the top of his head. It was Silk in his Fleetwood. He looked at Bruce and said, "You promise you won't scratch it?"

Big Bruce replied, "Yeah!" and hopped in the Cadi with Silk.

Big Bruce dropped Silk off at the car wash and then headed to Holly's house to get the gang. On his way to the house he saw Sand, Minnie, and some more girls walking to the jam at the I.L.A. Hall. He pulled the Fleetwood to the curb and asked, "Y'all going to the jam?"

Sand asked, "Silk know you got his car?"

Bruce replied, "Yeah!"

Minnie said, "He playing y'all?"

"Girl, he do know," Big Bruce replied. "Why, you want a ride?"

They all yelled, "Yeah, give us a ride!"

Bruce replied, "No!" and pulled away from the curb, leaving them behind.

When Big Bruce got to Holly's house, they all packed into the Fleetwood and headed to the jam. They all laughed when he told them how he pulled off on Champ's girl and her friends. He was always doing something crazy in order to get a laugh. When they made it to the jam, they were excited. There were cars everywhere. It seemed like the car owners had them waxed up just for the jam. There were girls everywhere, too. As they stared out the window, Donkey said, "I'ma get a lot of numbers tonight."

Big Bruce saw an empty spot on neutral grounds, and coasted the Cadi into it. Dusty spotted Redd's Cadi at the jam, too. He said, "Damn, look at Redd's Cadi over there!"

As they looked in the direction where Redd's Cadi was, Busty said, "Who is that driving his shit?"

They all got out steady, staring at Redd's Cadi. Then they noticed four guys in the car as it coasted by. Big Bruce took a good look at the driver and said, "Oh! That's Redd's nephew."

Dusty smacked his lips and asked, "How do you know?" as they all started walking to the entrance of the jam.

Big Bruce replied, "Because I met him at Redd's house once when I drove Silk over there. So shut up!"

Dusty mumbled, "Nigga, you shut up!"

There was a long line of people waiting to get in. It was almost a block away. As they started walking toward the end of the line, Champ heard somebody yelling, "Donkey! Bruce!"

It was his girl Kay and a few of her friends from her school. When Champ saw her it felt like he just wanted to die. Champ knew that Minnie and Sand were both coming because Bruce saw them; and now Kay and her friends had shown up.

Bo said, "Damn, Champ. Kay and Sand gon' be here. Nigga, you gon' get busted!"

Champ thought about what he said as they walked toward the front of the line where Kay was. Then he thought about what Silk had said about having to choose one day. As they walked past the line, a kid who was the star quarterback of the football team named Reggie Jones spoke to Donkey. Donkey gave him a firm handshake as they continued walking. A lot of people knew Donkey, but whenever they would talk about that he would just say that he had more enemies than friends.

When they got closer to the front of the line where Kay and her friends were, Kay walked up to Champ and gave him a warm, passionate kiss as her friends looked on. She then asked Champ how he got there. He said, "Silk let us use his Cadi. Why? How did y'all get here?"

Kay turned to point at one of her girlfriends and replied, "We are in my girlfriend's car." He looked at her friend who was caught up in a quick conversation with Busty. It was obvious that he was going to step to her and put his mack down. Champ tried to be as calm as possible in front of Kay, but deep inside he was going crazy trying to think of something to do. The line moved up and they got closer and closer to the entrance of the jam. Champ started to get nervous, and the whole gang knew it because he kept looking at them with uncertainty. Champ started to fiddle with the collar of his silk shirt as if it had become uncomfortable all of a sudden. He pulled his silk handkerchief from his back pocket and dabbed it across his forehead. Champ was beginning to perspire. He was caught between a rock and a hard place.

All of a sudden, Bo said, "Here come Minnie and the others now," and they looked. About a block and a half down the street, they saw Minnie, Sand and their friends walking toward the jam.

One of Kay's friends said, "Kay, just look at your sister. She thinks she is a woman." Kay started laughing, and Champ really started losing control. He started looking all around as if he was paranoid. He never noticed that one of Kay's friends was paying attention to him. She couldn't take her eyes off of him and he kept perspiring even more. He dabbed and dabbed his face with his silk handkerchief repeatedly. What was he going to do? Whom was he going to choose?

Then something unexpected happened. Bruce said, "Oh yeah, Champ! You forgot to lock up the office."

Champ looked at him with a curious expression. Then Dusty said, "Man, somebody might steal our stuff."

He glanced at Kay who was looking at him somewhat puzzled. "Man, you better hurry up." Big Bruce shouted as he tossed Champ the keys to the Fleetwood. Then he said, "Go ahead, man!"

Champ stared at the Fleetwood keys in his hand. He didn't know what Big Bruce and Dusty were up to, but he was with it anyway. He turned to Kay, gave her a kiss, said, "I'll be right back," and ran to the Fleetwood. He cranked it up and left. One of Kay's girlfriends asked her, "Girl, where is he going?" as they watched the Fleetwood race up the block.

She replied, "He'll be back."

After leaving the jam, Champ had nowhere to go. He wasn't going to ride around all night, so he went to the car wash, tossed Silk his keys, and explained to him why he wasn't at the jam. The first thing that Silk said was, "I told you so!"

While everybody was at the jam, Silk and Champ sat in his office watching movies. It was about ten thirty or a quarter to eleven and the movie that were on had become a bore to him. So Champ decided to go outside and roam through the hood for a while. Silk figured that since everybody else was at the jam, the least he could do was let Champ drive the Fleetwood for the rest of the night.

That night, Champ drove down every street in his neighborhood. He had the windows up and the A/C on high. He was listening to one of Silk's tapes called The Isley Brothers. He passed over by the Fruit Man's house on Dorgenois Street. The Fruit Man sold puffies out of his house for two dollars, so Champ picked up a couple. Back in the

Fleetwood, he had the music on and the A/C was still flowing. He lit up a puffie and was smoking it while leaning to the side. He was trying to drive the Cadi like Silk use to do.

Champ felt like he ruled the world that night. He came up to M.L.K. to Galvez and took a left on the corner of the projects. He went straight up Galvez for three blocks and took a left turn. At the third street, he went one block to a stop sign at Johnson. There were a couple of winos standing out in front of a closed grocery store called Salem. They watched him coast across the intersection. They both waved at the Cadi as he passed, thinking that he was Silk. Champ tapped the horn twice and started smiling. As he came to the middle of the block, he saw Bianca, Donkey's baby momma, sitting on the steps by herself and chilling. He stopped the car in front of her house and rolled down the window, letting the entire reefer smoke blow out. He asked her, "Why you ain't at the jam?"

She replied, "I had to watch my baby."

He took a puff off of the reefer and said, "You should have gotten somebody to watch him."

She hunched her shoulders and said, "Give me some of that!"

He knew that Bianca got high because she usually did that with Donkey. Champ said, "Hold up! Let me park." He pulled the Fleetwood to the curb. After he parked the car, he walked back to Bianca's steps, sat next to her, and shared the puffie with her. While they were getting high, she said something to him that caught him off guard. She said, "Champ, I know about you" as he passed the puffie back to her.

Champ said, "What do you know about me?"

She took a puff of the reefer and said, "You know. About Kay and Sand."

His eyes widened in shock. He asked her, "What about Kay and Sand?" thinking that he could throw her off.

She replied, "You don't have to act like that! I ain't gon' say nothing," as she passed the reefer back to him. He stared at her, trying to figure out why she was telling him this. Then she looked at him and just stared for a while. She stood up, opened her screen door, and said, "Come on, let's go inside," and without hesitation, he got up and followed her into her house.

For the first time since Champ had known Bianca, he thought about having sex with her. Kay, Sand, and not even Donkey were on his mind at this time. Bianca grabbed him by his wrist and led him through her house to her bedroom. They passed by her momma's room, and Champ could see her momma with Lil' Herman cuddled in her arms. He was sound asleep.

When they got to her room, she told him to relax as she closed the door. He sat down on her queen-sized bed and waited. His john felt like it wanted to burst out of its skin. She picked up a shirt off her dresser and walked through another room that led to the bathroom. She stayed in there for about a minute or two, and then she came out with her shorts and blouse in her hands.

It was obvious to Champ that she wasn't wearing a bra because the print of her nipples poked out through the shirt. She placed the clothes in a small basket on the side of her dresser, and walked over to the television. She started browsing the channels. Then she said, "You know what, Champ?" as she stood with her back turned toward him.

He then also noticed that she didn't have any panties on as he said, "What's that?"

She turned to him and pulled off her shirt, revealing her perfectly naked body. She replied, "I know you ain't never did this before," and then she walked over and grabbed his hand and placed it between her legs so that he could feel the lips of her vagina. She was dripping wet already. He slipped his finger into her pussy and felt the warmth of her insides. She let out a light moaning sound. She grabbed his hands and put them on her breasts. He squeezed them gently, as if he knew what he was doing. She then pushed him back to lie on the bed. She unbuttoned his pants, pulled off his shoes and then pulled off his pants. Champ's boxers were next to come off. She looked his cock, as it stood straight up, fully erect. He sat up to take his silk shirt off, but she started to unbutton it and take it off herself. When she finished, she also removed his undershirt. He lied on the bed, and she crawled on top of him. She put his hands on her waist and she grabbed his cock to position it upward. Then she slowly lowered her body down for him to ease into her. She rotated it around a little bit trying to find the precise spot. She stopped and started moving her body up and down at a very slow pace.

Bianca knew exactly what she wanted to do; she wanted to be the first to take advantage of Champ's virginity. She kept moving her body in the same style, over and over. She made a lot of low cries like, "Oooh! Yeah!" and then, "I'm cumming! I'm cumming!" As she started to move faster and faster with longer cries, Champ found himself drifting off into his mind.

He was thinking about when he was young and how he used to listen to his momma make the same cries when Mr. Henry came over, but the cries were louder then. He also thought about the time when he peeped into his momma's room and saw Mr. Henry on her. They were butt naked on the bed. All of a sudden, he felt a smack in his chest and it brought him back out of his daze. He asked, "Why did you hit me?"

She replied, "You ain't cum yet?"

Champ looked down at his cock and it was still pointing

upward and erect. "Don't look like it," he said.

She got up off the bed, walked over to the dresser, got her a shirt, and put it on. "Look, we gon' have to do this another time, cause I have been up there trying to get you to cum for damn near an hour, and I am tired."

As he started slipping on his clothes she said, "Tomorrow, we gon' stay from school. When my momma go to work you come over here and we gon' do it right."

Champ replied, "Alright." He got dressed and she walked him to the door. After he left, he went straight to Holly's house, took a bath, and was smiling from ear to ear because he had gotten him some draws. He made two, peanut butter and jelly sandwiches, got himself a glass of milk, ate them and went straight to sleep.

CHAPTER FOUR

When Champ woke up it was the next morning. Big Bruce was shaking him, telling him to wake up because everybody was dressed for school except for him. He looked up at him, wiped his eyes, and said, "Man, I ain't going today!"

Bruce yelled, "Man, it's the second day of school. What 'cha mean you ain't going?"

Champ knew that he couldn't tell him the real reason why he wasn't going to school, so he thought of a quick lie to tell him. "Holly is gon' take me on down to the hospital. She thinks that I come down with the flu." He put an expression on his face as if he was sick.

Bruce looked at him for a moment and then said, "Ah, nigga, you just don't want them hoes to see you. But you can stay here." Then he picked up his empty book bag and said, "We are going to school and gon' put our mack down," as he left the room.

Champ heard him in the front telling the gang that he was sick and couldn't go to school. It was on when he heard the door slam shut. He called Bianca's house and told her that he was on his way, and that he would be knocking at her front door in twenty minutes.

They started fucking at about a quarter to nine. Bianca leaned over forward with her hands while holding on to the dresser. Champ stood behind her with his cock jammed inside her pussy, stroking it repeatedly back and forth. She screamed out his name in a loud moan, "Oooh, Champ! Oooh!" as he continued to stroke.

She got down on the floor and put her legs up on his shoulders, while he stroked her long and easy. They had a nice lovemaking tempo going. Every time his cock erected they were in a different position. After it was all said and done, Champ realized he liked it the traditional way the best.

At 11:35 they were lying in bed, butt naked with just a sheet covering their lower bodies. She rested her head on his chest as they watched the daytime soaps. Bianca said to him, "I don't know how Donkey will handle this," as she ran her hands across his chest. "You ever thought about that?"

That's when Champ started picturing how it would turn out. He shook his head in the negative, and then she said, "The last thing I want to do is hurt him." All was silent for a minute. The only thing that was heard was the soap opera. Then she broke the silence by saying, "Champ, if it came down to it, who would you pick?"

He knew that she was talking about Kay and Sand so he replied, "I'll take them both."

"Ain't no woman gon' share her man. I don't know what is taking you so long to fuck 'em."

He shouted angrily, "Why you worried about that?"

Bianca rose up from under the sheet, showing her full, firm breasts and yelled, "Cause you ain't doing nothing but getting them ready for the next nigga!"

He just stared at her, because he knew then that she had something on her mind. Why he hadn't fucked Sand or Kay yet wasn't it by a long shot. So he said, "What are you trying to say?"

Then Champ noticed that the wells of her eyes had flooded with tears, and then one tear slowly rolled down the side of her face as she began to cry. "They just playing wit 'cho mind, Champ. Your mind," as she got out of the bed and ran into the bathroom.

He called out her name and asked her to open the door, and she spoke in a low tone, telling him to leave. He didn't want to leave things the way that they were, so he said, "Come on, Bianca. Open the door!"

"Just leave, Champ!" she shouted, "All I want you to do is leave!" He stood by the bathroom door for a few minutes, and then he realized that her mind was set on not opening the door. He slipped on his clothes and left.

After he left Bianca's house, he went home and thought that he would chill until the gang came home from school. It was 12:27 PM when he looked at the clock, so he didn't have but a few hours to wait. He thought about everything he and Bianca had shared together: the sex, and the conversation. He thought about what she had said about Sand and Kay messing with his mind. He thought about what she said about him getting them ready for another nigga. Then he wondered if he should believe her or not. He also thought about how long he had been with the both of them. Was it a coincidence that he had not fucked either of them in five years? Then he asked himself if he really loved them. He thought that he did. He also asked himself if he could live without them, or maybe without one of them. He would have to sleep on that question, so he lay back on the sofa for a few minutes and dozed off.

Later on that evening after the gang had come home from school, they were all at the car wash making money. Champ was in Silk's office talking to him about women. Silk said to him, "Champ," as he sipped on a soda, "it's no way I can school you on a broad because a broad is hard to understand."

Champ said to him, "Just tell me why they make you wait so long to fuck?"

He starting laughing and said, "Women have the tendency to play games with yo mind." He continued to sip on his soda. "They'll sometimes hold back on the pussy in order to see how much you love them, or if you love them at all." Champ thought about that for a while and came up with a solution. He figured if Sand and Kay were waiting to have sex with him to see how much he loved them, then he wanted to know how much they loved him, too.

He walked around the corner to Kay's house where she and a couple of her friends were hanging out in the front. As he approached her porch, her friends yelled, "Hey, Champ!"

But he totally ignored them, because even though he was Kay's boyfriend, her friends still looked at him as a little boy because of his age. He looked at Kay and said, "I am ready to fuck."

They were all shocked at what he had said. He knew that she was embarrassed because he said that in front of her friends. He wanted to see how she would handle it. She was hiding something. He knew it, because she was acting too jolly all of a sudden. To be honest, he felt like she was trying to make him look small. When he asked her what was she going to do, she starting grinning and then replied, "I'ma think about it."

Champ just stared at her and then they all started laughing. He looked at her friends with an angry frown on his face and when they noticed that he didn't find it funny, they stopped laughing. He looked at Kay and said, "While you are thinking about it, I may be moving on. I hope you don't have a problem with that." Then he turned around and left.

As he was leaving, he heard one of her friends say, "Damn, Kay! What's wrong with him?"

Kay smacked her lips and fanned him off while saying, "Girl, Champ a Lil' boy! His ass gon' be calling me tonight apologizing."

After leaving Kay's house Champ really starting believing everything that Bianca had said to him. In the beginning he just wanted to see if she had any feelings for him. But since things turned out the way that they did, he figured that he'd play the player in a game of his own. He knew that there were a lot of broads who liked him. There were a lot of girls with whom he could put his mack down. Worrying about a female was a waste of time.

That night after he got home, Holly said, "Champ! That girl has been calling for you all night. I told her that you was at work, and she still call right back!"

He asked, "Who, Kay?" as he stood in the doorway of her bedroom.

She yelled, "No! It's Sand. All damn day!" Then she began to mimic Sand, "Champ there? Champ there?"

Champ knew that he had to call her because it had been forty-eight hours since he had talked to her. He walked over, picked up the phone from the foot of her bed, and called Sand. The last time that he had spoken to her, an old lady was chasing them from in front of her house with a broom in her hand. He started to dial the number when it dawned on him that Sand wasn't any different from Kay. The phone rang, and his mind began to drift off in space. Then he heard someone say, "Hello?"

Champ said, "Who is this?"

She said, "It's Sand." He remained silent, and she began to yell, "Hello!" and then he hung up.

The next day at school Sand asked him in front of the whole class, "Yo' sister ain't tell you that I was calling for you?"

He replied, "Yeah, but I was busy."

She continued, "But you could have called me and said someth-"

"Look!" He yelled, cutting her off. The whole class got quiet and looked towards the back of the room where they were sitting. "I said I was busy! Now I don't want to talk about it."

Ms. Watkins shouted, "Mr. Randolph and Miss Watson, if you are having problems that don't concern American History then you should settle that outside of this classroom!"

Sand stared at Champ, and he knew that she was angry. Donkey turned around to see what was going on. He looked in the front of the class at Ms. Watkins and mumbled, "Man, let me get the fuck outta here." Champ got up from his desk and walked out. He left the whole class in suspense because he walked out at 8:43 AM. He went to the car wash and chilled out with Silk.

After school, something crazy happened. Big Bruce walked around to Kay's auntie's house and asked to speak to her. When she came outside, he asked her, "What's going on between you and my boy?"

Kay looked at him and said, "That ain't your business" as she put her hands on her hips and spoke with a loud tone.

Big Bruce started to get angry and said, "Well, bitch. That's my boy and I'ma make it my business!"

Kay then looked at him and started to get nervous, as she noticed him getting upset. The sound of his voice frightened her. She spoke in a low tone as she stuttered, "W-w-we just don't talk no more."

Big Bruce just stood there and stared into space for a while. Then he asked, "After five years?" and Kay nodded. Big Bruce looked up one block and then down the other, and then back at Kay. He said, "I'd go out over my dog getting hurt. I just thought you ought to know" and then he left.

Kay stared at him as he walked away. She went inside, closed the door behind her, and started laughing, saying, "Them Lil' boys is a trip." She then went into her room, picked up the telephone and dialed a number and said, "Girl! Let me tell you what just happened."

Later on that day at the car wash, Silk was on the phone asking Redd to have a good friend of his lend him a favor.

About an hour before, Busty and Big Bruce were delivering a package for Silk in the Melphomene Projects. It was two and a half grams of heroin. They were caught by Narcotic agents and arrested for "Possession with Intent to Distribute." To make matters worse, since they were juveniles the only way they could be released was if a senior judge approved of it. Redd had a friend in Criminal Court named Leonard who was associated with lawyers and judges throughout the state. There was a time when Silk was arrested for heroin up in Pasadena, California. He was picking up a large package for his cousin, Gator. Gator in turn introduced Silk to Redd, who had him out easy with help from Leonard. Yet, Leonard didn't like the idea of being associated with juveniles, so there was nothing that Redd could do to help them.

That night, for some reason cars kept pulling into the car wash so Silk let it stay open after closing time because this had never happened before. It was only Bo, Donkey, Dusty, and Champ working, since Busty and Big Bruce were in the Juvenile Center.

Champ had just finished up on a pretty banana yellow Pontiac Grand Prix and was putting his things back in my bucket to get ready for the next car.

Then a black Camaro with centerline rims, dual exhaust, tinted windows and a scoop hood pulled up in my area. Champ walked over to the driver side and tapped on the window. He told the driver that he could walk over to the seating area near the office if he chose to. The window rolled down slowly and when it did, Champ had the shock of his life. He saw Kay's ex-boyfriend, Damien, behind the wheel, and Kay seated across from him on the passenger side. They both looked Champ dead in his eyes. Kay had a sassy look on her face, and he was chewing on a stick of gum. Champ looked in the back seat and there were her friends Brenda and Reggie Jones, the star quarterback of the football team. Damien says to Champ, "Just wipe it down, Lil' man."

Champ looked at him with fire burning in his eyes. He was trying to portray the role of a baller. Champ had flashes of lifting him out of his car and kicking his ass. Instead, he just said, "Alright, just a wipe down," as he stepped away from the car.

Damien began to roll his window back up and Champ overheard Reggie saying, "Lil' Daddy act like he don't want to wash cars."

He wiped the Camaro down and then knocked on the window for the money. Kay just stared at Champ as Damien dug in his pocket for the money. He came out of his pocket with a large roll of money and flipped through it while saying, "Damn, I know I got some tens in here," as he look back at Reggie. Then he said, "Reg, you got some tens in your pocket?"

Reg replied, "Naw D'!"

Champ started laughing and said, "Look, give me a twenty and I will run to get you some change."

He looked at Champ and said, "Naw. I'll tell you what." He handed me the twenty dollar bill and said, "You go ahead and keep the change, Lil' man. It's cool." Champ grabbed the money and they pulled off.

Even though he knew that Damien was trying to make himself look big, Champ still took the money because he was bigger. That meant he wasn't a fool by a long shot. After they, left Champ went back to work and later on that night they returned. This time, the driver side window was already rolled down and only Damien and Reggie were in the car. Damien asked Champ, "Lil' man, won't you run on over there and tell Donkey that D' Man want to holla' at him?" and Champ looked at him trying to figure out why would he want to see Donkey.

Reggie said, "It's cool." Then Champ remembered Donkey kicking it with him, so he figured that it was all right. He walked over to Donkey, who was drying off a Cadillac Seville, and told him who wanted him.

Before he walked away, Champ asked him, "What's going on?" with concern.

Donkey replied, "Just chill." He walked over to the Camaro, got in, and they drove off.

When they returned, Donkey got out and they drove off again. Champ walked over to him and asked, "What was all that about?"

He acted as if he didn't want to discuss it, but said, "Oh, it ain't nothing."

Champ wanted Donkey to tell him more, so he insisted, "Come on, nigga. Let a nigga know what's up!"

He looked at Champ and said, "Wha' cha tripping on?" Then he said, "It's cool, Champ. It's cool" and left it like that.

At about 11:30 PM, they were closing up the car wash and getting ready to go inside when Redd pulled up. Champ figured that he and Silk would sit in the office, smoke a reefer, and talk about money until dawn. But it wasn't one of those times. Redd had come to talk to Champ.

He parked his Cadi under the fifth cover, and called over to Champ as he got out and sat on the hood. As he was walking toward Redd, he could feel him staring at him. He told Champ, "Come and chill out with old Redd, and let me put a bug in your ear." Champ was shaking like the hood on a '57 Chevy because he had no idea what Redd wanted to talk to him about. He lit up a reefer, hit it twice then passed it over to Champ and said, "Lil' man, I don't usually get into these Lil' kiddie games. However, whenever my baby girl ain't smiling," and he reached for the reefer, "I know something is wrong. So what's up with you and Sand?"

Champ started choking on the smoke from the reefer,

because he was caught by surprise with that one. Champ's eyes opened wide and he said, "Everything is cool," and then he pounded his chest for relief.

"Come on now, Lil' man. Be true with old Redd. I know when something is wrong with my baby," and as Redd continued, he took another hit off the reefer. "What's going on? Y'all ain't seeing each other no more, is that it?"

Champ didn't know what to say, and he didn't want to lie to him so he just went on and told him the truth. He said, "Man! I don't know what is going on."

Redd passed him the reefer. Champ hit it and continued, "See, I don't know what I want to do, bro" and he turned to look Redd in his eyes.

"You putting your mack down on another squeeze, are ya not?"

Redd reminded Champ of his Pops when he said that, and he replied, "You know about the squeeze and all?" and he nodded his head.

Then Champ told him the truth about that, too. He told him that he liked them both and that Silk had told him that he was gonna have to choose one day so he figure that before he chose, he would leave them both alone.

Redd just stared at Champ for a while and then he said, "Well, I can respect that. I just wanted to see which way the ball was rolling, Lil' Man," and he got off of the hood of his car. As he stood on the ground, he looked back and then said, "Yeah! Me and you never talked about this. And tell Silk I'ma holla at him later." He got in his car, cranked it up and left.

CHAPTER FIVE

The next day, everything was a panic. It seemed as if the worst thing that could happen to Champ picked that very day and time to actually happen. He was on bad terms with both of his girls. Then, Busty and Big Bruce got sent to the Detention Center. They couldn't come home. Yet the worst of all the news was that somebody had kidnapped his girl, Sand.

They took her from her house and demanded that Redd come up with the ransom. If he didn't, they would kill Sand. Redd yelled at Silk, "Where the fuck we gon' get five hundred thousand dollars from?" He paced Silk's office back and forth. "I got two hundred," he shouted "and you got one and a quarter. We still short a hundred and seventy five grand!"

Then Silk made a suggestion, "We can get the rest from the boys?" as he sat behind his desk in his wheelchair.

Redd shook his head and said, "It ain't a spot in the city that can make that much in a day!" and he continued to pace the office. "Maybe if you tell them three an a quarter an eleven zones, they'll go with it," said Redd. The entire office was quiet for a moment.

"But Silk, that's everything," Redd let out a defeated, ragged sigh. Silk looked into Redd's bloodshot eyes and said, "Priceless."

Redd took a deep breath, closed his eyes and lowered his head in despair. He felt as if he had the whole world sitting up on his shoulders. Besides getting his baby girl back, he was also thinking about what it took him to get where he was. He could never picture himself doing it again. He raised his head, looked at Silk and said, "I guess we gotta do it." So

Redd made a phone call from Silk's office to whoever it was that had kidnaped Sand and said, "I know that this is not the deal, but it is all that I can come up with" and he told them what he had.

After a minute or two, the other party agreed to take what he had. They set up a place to do the transaction for an hour later. Redd got off the phone and told Silk that they had agreed. Redd said that he was going to pick up the money from his house and he was coming right back.

When he rushed out to his car and left, Silk called the boys into his office. When they got there, he was loading up his Army forty-five. When he finished, he sat it on his desk. He opened up the desk drawer, pulled out another magazine, and sat it beside the gun. He turned to look at the gang with deadpan, serious eyes. "Y'all look here," he took a deep breath. "Me and Redd is going to take care of some business." Then he looked at Champ and said, "Serious business. We don't know how things gon' turn out, so if I don't come back, y'all take care of the car wash! And handle y'all business! Ya'll hear?"

Silk rested back in his wheelchair and they nodded, letting him know that they felt him and they were okay. It felt like they were at a funeral. Dusty asked, "If you don't think that you are coming back, then why are you going?"

Silk looked at Dusty and said, "It's all in the game, Lil' Dee. A scary gambler will never win. Now y'all go ahead out there and do what y'all was doing and if anybody pull up tell them that the car wash is closed for the day." The gang all walked out of his office.

Not long after that, Redd returned. He wasn't alone. He had the Fruit Man and Mr. Charlie the barber along with him. They all got out of Redd's Cadi and walked into the office. When they came out, Charlie the Barber carried Silk in his arms. He put him in the car and they left. Champ didn't even want to imagine how many guns were in that car.

Redd was told to meet somebody at the Louisiana Street Wharf at the river. He sat in the back passenger side seat with three hundred and twenty five thousand dollars and eleven ounces of pure heroin in a duffle bag, and a .44 Magnum in his lap. The Fruit Man sat across from him with a sawed-off gun laid across his lap. In the front seat, Silky Slim sat on the passenger side with a .44 in his hand. Since Silk was paralyzed, he had taken something that he could handle easily. Driving the car was Charlie the Barber. He had a Mossberg pump laid across his lap. If they were stopped by the cops for some reason, they wouldn't ever see daylight again.

As they neared the Wharf, they all did what they had to do to make sure their weapons were ready. They pulled up to the corner of Louisiana and Tchopitoulas. They looked straight ahead to the entrance of the Wharf. A fella stood just inside the entrance signaling for them to come inside. Charlie the Barber pulled the car inside the Wharf gate, slowly. So far, everything was clean. They pulled past the entrance gate about twenty-five yards and then stopped and looked around. They were trying to place the gunmen.

Silky Slim said, "I got one on the roof just ahead!"

Charlie the Barber said, "I got 'em, and I also got one about twenty yards behind the tractor." Redd's eyes went to the tractor. They did everything without head movements.

Fruit Man said, "I got two rifles on the top ship." All eyes focused on the ship, where two riflemen were crouched behind some wooden crates.

Slim said, "I've got a Cre' in a Continental. It's just behind us on your right side. And two cars off the corner," as he looked through his rear-view mirror.

Just then a fella showed up from the corner of one of the

warehouses, and then another one from just a few feet behind him. The first guy had a tight grip on one of Sand's arms and in his other hand, a pistol. Redd opened the door of the car, got out and walked towards them. The .44 Magnum was in his back waistline. The duffle bag stayed in the car. As he approached, the first man asked, "Where is the money?"

He ignored the man while he looked at a terrified, crying Sand and said, "Let her walk to the car and you get yo' money," Redd snarled. Redd looked at the first guy who held onto Sand. He stood about five feet behind the second guy, who stood about five feet from Redd. The first guy looked at Redd cautiously and then to the car. He thought about it. When he looked back at Redd, Redd stared right into his eyes. Redd saw pure fear.

Finally, the first guy agreed and ordered the second guy to let Sand go by giving him a hand signal. Sand started walking toward the passenger side of the car, and as she neared the car, all of the windows rolled down. She got to the window where Silky Slim sat and told her to stop. He looked into her eyes with a deadly serious look and said slowly, "When I say go, I want you to get in the trunk and lay down as low as you can, okay?"

When the back passenger door opened, Silky Slim cocked the hammer on the .45. The Fruit Man got out of the car slowly with the duffle bag in his right hand, raised his head, and had his left hand on the shotgun that stuck halfway out the car. The Fruit Man's gun couldn't be seen by anyone but the guys in the Continental behind them. Silky Slim opened the glove compartment, and pushed a button that opened the trunk.

It all happened in seconds. Charlie the Barber cocked the Mossberg, grabbed the handle of the door, and opened it. Slim yelled, "GO!" while sticking the .45 out the window and hitting the button for the trunk.

Sand ran to the trunk and the Fruit Man came up and shot the gun. They all depended on that shot because he was the first one to get a clear one. Then he aimed at the second guy and shot. Sand hopped into the trunk and laid low. The shot hit the second guy in the chest, and the impact knocked him back about ten feet. At the same time, Redd rushed the first guy who had pulled out his pistol and they both began a tussle for life. Redd shoved him away from the gun, while grabbing hold of it. The guy fell to the ground and Redd stood over him and put five bullets in his chest. "Nigga, I'm Dirty Redd!" he yelled.

Suddenly, a bullet from one of the gunmen struck Redd in the shoulder and knocked him to the ground. Charlie the Barber started pacing his way toward him while trying to hit the rifleman on top. Silky Slim fired shots at the rifleman repeatedly. They weren't being hit, but it was buying them some time. Besides, they couldn't get a good shot without escaping a bullet. Then there was a shot from behind.

The four guys in the Continental were opening fire. The Fruit Man turned around and started blasting at them as he slammed the trunk of the car down. He dropped one, then another, but then he got hit by a rifleman. One to his side and one near a kidney, and then he fell to the ground. The duffle bag flew about twenty feet away as the Fruit Man fell. Charlie the Barber couldn't hold on to Redd and shoot the Mosberg at the same time, so they made it the best way they could. Redd held his arm around Charlie the Barber's neck as tight as he could, as they paced back to the car. When Redd got to the car, he noticed that the Fruit Man wasn't there. He yelled, "Kyle!" and Charlie the Barber started looking around. He was looking for the Fruit Man.

The Mosberg was empty so Charlie yelled, "Gun!" and Silk handed him his .45. Charlie the Barber ran around to the other side of the car, shooting until he found the Fruit Man.

He was bleeding fast. Charlie shot at the two guys still in the Continental and then ran for cover so he could help the Fruit Man into the car. It worked, and with that, he believed he was better than they were at gun fighting, because the others ran for cover. He helped the Fruit Man into the back seat of the car, slammed the door, let off a few more shots at the other men to hold them off a little longer, and got into the car without closing the door. He put the car in reverse and punched on the accelerator. As the car moved backward, it rolled over one of the wounded gunmen who were lying in the street. He stopped the car, threw it in drive, and then peeled off down Tchopitolas Street, heading to Charity Hospital.

After Silk told the boys about that night, none of them could sleep. All of them feared that Silk was going to get killed, so they all waited for the news to come in. At ten o'clock, the nightly news came on and it hit them hard. The news anchor reported that four men had been killed in a drug deal gone wrong. They said that investigators confiscated a large amount of cash, along with a large amount of heroin valued at nearly a half a million dollars. There were no suspects at this time. The gang all stared at the television, even after they were through talking about it, with tears rolling down all of their faces.

Everything Silk had done for the boys started crossing their minds. They all went to bed and cried themselves to sleep. The next morning, they headed to the car wash. It seemed as if the closer they got to the car wash, the more everything felt like the last time Silk got shot and almost died. As the boys walked past the fruit stand, they noticed that it was closed, just like last time. The barbershop was closed, too, and it was the same way at the car wash. There was no sign of Silk, so they had to open the car wash on their own. Usually, Bruce would have a second key. However, since he was away at the Detention Center, Silk had made Champ a key. He opened it up and they got ready for business.

At about one o'clock, the cars started rolling in and the boys went to work. At about three o'clock, Champ had finished a pearl-white Monte Carlo with a white leather exterior, and he thought that he would chill out for a minute. Champ went into the office and looked around a bit. He found himself behind Silk's desk, sitting in his wheelchair. He didn't want to end up in one, but he just sat there thinking about Silk. He placed his hand on the wheels and twisted the chair around in a circle, just like Silk use to do when he wanted to be alone. Champ sat straight up, rested his arms on the desk, and thought about what Silk had told them about the game. How he showed Champ and Donkey how to operate an automatic pistol. He looked at the clock on the wall and it was 3:18 pm. Champ realized that he was really going to miss Silk.

All of a sudden, the door of the office swung open and Charlie the Barber walked, in carrying Silky Slim in his arms. He looked at Champ and said, "Get outta my chair, Lil' nigga. Ol' Silk ain't gone nowhere!"

Champ started smiling and got out of the chair. Charlie sat him down in the chair and said, "Silk, this Lil' nigga was up in here reminiscing."

The gang rushed into the office and saw Silk. Everyone began to smile and Dusty said, "Welcome home, Silk!" He thought about what they had talked about before, about the family thing.

Silk replied, "And I'm glad to be here."

For the next three days after Silk came back everything was normal, except for one thing: there wasn't anything being sold. Whenever someone came to score, Silk told the boys to tell them that the shop was closed, or it ain't nothing.

They missed out on three days of work and a lot of money that could have been made. Champ thought that was the reason why Silk spent most of his time on the phone. Redd would come over sometimes and scoop him up in his girl's car and they would leave. Champ always wondered why he didn't drive his Cadi anymore.

One day, Silk called the gang in the office because he said that he needed to talk to them about something. When they were all settled in the office, he began by saying, "I got some good news, and I got some bad news." He looked around to make sure he had their full attention, and continued. "The good news is y'all know that the Fruit Man got into a little accident, right?" Again, he made sure they were listening before he continued. "Well, he made a successful recovery, and he'll be back at the fruit stand in a little while."

Then he took a deep breath and said, "Now for the bad news." He looked as if someone had died. "Fellas, old Silk gon' have to close the car wash." They were silent, initially. All of them were shocked.

Donkey said, "Silk, you can't close the car wash!"

"I'm sorry, Fellas," Silk replied. "But even though the shop gon' be closed, old Silk still gon' be hanging around," he said, cracking a smile.

Bo asked, "Why you closing it?"

Silk turned to him and said, "Because I don't have any more money to keep it up, and nothing to make money with." That one statement put a lot of things into action without any of them really knowing it yet.

That's when Donkey asked, "Well, how much do you need?"

"I got house notes, car notes, notes on the shop, utilities. I need this and I need that. I got hospital bills," he took a deep breath. After a short pause, Silk continued, "I need a package to satisfy my customers. The shop needs wax soap, sponges, tire cleaner, detergent, and towels." Silk stopped and looked at them. "Hell, I can't even get y'all new uniforms. We are talking about dollars right now." Then he turned to Donkey and said, "Now, am I getting my point across?"

Donkey left the car wash, went to Holly's house, got the money that they had stored away and came back to the office with it in a bag. He slammed one hundred and ten thousand dollars down on top of Silk's desk. Then Donkey asked, "Is this enough?"

Silk was in shock as he looked at the large stacks of money on his desk, "Oh, yeah. More than enough," as he reached out to gather it. As Silk put his hand on the money, Champ put his hand on top of the money and said, "Silk, promise us that you'll get Bruce and Busty out of the Detention Center."

Silk stared into Champ's eyes and at that moment, he truly realized that the gang's safety, wealth, and freedom meant the world to him. He replied, "Sure, Champ. I promise." Champ removed his hands from the top of the stack of money and then slid it over to Silk.

After that day, money slid across the desk on a regular basis. Redd talked to his friend, Leonard, and he put his neck on a chopping block to get Bruce and Busty out. The car wash was back to normal. They were back in business full force.

Two weeks later, the boys were pulling in a little bit under $16,500 a day. In one week, we made $82,000 to $115,000. Redd and Silk both thought there was too much money lying around. They opened up an account in a large bank downtown.

One morning, when the boys had all arrived at the car wash, Redd and Silk had done something to show their appreciation for what they had done for them. They had purchased five, brand-new Cadillacs. One was cherry red, one was midnight blue, another was jet black, the next emerald green, and the fifth one was pearl-white. Each had matching leather exterior and a vinyl top. There were five, but Busty couldn't drive just yet. Busty took the blue one to store until he could drive; Bo took the white one; Bruce the red one; Donkey selected the green one; and that left Champ with the dope black one.

They got their own apartment in Kenner. Bo and Champ furnished their mom's, Ms. Katt's, and Holly's apartments. Minnie moved in with Bo, and Bianca moved in with Donkey. Busty, Dusty and Big Bruce was fucking any fly female that was down with giving up the nappy dugout. As for Champ, every now and then he'd get together with Bianca on the lowdown. He never stopped asking, and she never started saying no. By this time, they knew more about the game than ever. They learned how to test, weigh, bag, and cut heroin; if you would have told anyone that they were only fifteen, they would not have believed you.

Back at school, it was the same. Champ hadn't spoken to Sand or Kay in over a month. Sand had her schedule changed so she was no longer in any of his classes. One day, Champ was in the cafeteria eating with Corey Bernard and Isaac Bell, who were in his third period class. He knew Corey by meeting him at Donkey's cousin Herman's house. Isaac was the star point guard on the basketball team. Champ started liking Corey because he was a good comedian like Big Bruce. As for Isaac, he was always putting his mack down on the females like Champ. They were sitting at the table eating when Isaac asked, "When we gon' hit the club, nigga? I mean, you got a fresh-ass Cadi and shit."

"Maybe Friday when I get off," Champ replied. He continued to dress his hamburger with ketchup and mayonnaise.

Corey said, "Say Champ! It ain't true about what they say, is it?"

Champ slapped the burger together and then replied, "I don't know. What they say?" He bit down on the burger.

Corey said, "That you work at a car wash."

Everybody at the table stopped what they were doing to hear what Champ had to say, so he stopped chewing and then said, "What? You never seen a nigga work at a car wash before?"

Everybody went back to doing what they were doing, and Champ picked up a French fry from his tray and stuck it in his mouth. That's when Champ noticed this girl seated three tables across from him, staring. She had brown skin, long, jet-black hair that was in a ponytail, and she looked good; damn good. Isaac noticed Champ staring at her. Then Champ asked, "Who is she?"

"Oh! That's LaToya Winnsboro, and you can just forget about that because she is off limits," Corey said.

Champ looked at the both of them and then said, "First of all, you ain't no mack, Corey," and the whole table started laughing. "I don't know what makes her any different from any other broad," said Champ. He looked down to the other end of the table where four senior females were eating their lunch and said, "Say you on the end!" The whole table looked down at the girl on the other end of the table as she looked at him and he asked, "How do you think I look?"

She starting blushing and was smiling from ear to ear as she replied, "You look good."

And Champ turned and looked at Isaac, and said, "Now that's putting your mack down!"

After school was out, Champ walked to the schoolyard and realized that the gang must've left early, because their cars were gone. As he walked to his car, somebody yelled out, "Say you!" Champ turned around and saw a red bone approaching him.

As she approached him, she said, "You don't take no time getting out of here, do you?"

"No, I have to go to work," and as Champ looked at her, he noticed that she had beautiful hazel eyes, like Sand.

"Do you have any idea how popular you are here?" she asked. She put on the prettiest smile and said, "Let's do this again. Hi, my name is LaToya and I'm the captain of the cheerleaders."

"Well, my name is Champ and I wash cars." She stared at Champ and then looked over at his Cadillac and said, "That's a joke, right?"

He replied, "No! It ain't no joke."

All of a sudden, someone yelled, "Hey!"

They both looked toward the building where two guys were running toward them, and LaToya mumbled, "Ah, shit!"

Champ asked her who they were and she replied, "That's my boyfriend and his boy."

As they approached Champ and LaToya, her boyfriend asked, "Who the fuck is this nigga?"

"We just running over some questions for the pop quiz in Ms. Anderson's class tomorrow," she said.

"Shut up!" he yelled, shoved her aside and stepped closer to Champ. "Look here, nigga, find you another bitch because this one is taken," and he shoved Champ back on to his Cadillac.

Champ shoved him back and said, "Maybe you ought a check your bitch, nigga!"

He attempted to come at Champ again, but his friend grabbed him and held him back saying, "Be cool Jay, be cool."

Jay replied, "Yeah! I'ma be cool." Then he pointed at Champ, "But you better stay the fuck out of my way!" They walked away with LaToya following behind. Champ got in his car and left.

Later at the car wash, Champ couldn't get what had happened in the schoolyard off of his mind. Busty saw that something was bothering him, and took it upon himself to ask Champ what was happening. He told Busty that everything was cool, and Busty just stared at Champ for a while. Then he said, "Man, you can't let 'em keep you down, Bro!"

Champ looked surprised as he thought to himself, *How could he possibly know about the incident in the school yard?* So Champ asked him, "Wha'cha talkin' 'bout?"

He pulled a puffie out of his pocket while saying, "Man! Look here, just forget it, Bro, because we about to light up this reefer."

"No nigga! Wha'cha talkin' 'bout?" Champ yelled, with an angry expression over his face.

It was then that Busty realized that something was on Champ's mind, "No doubt" he replied, "Don't start tripping, Champ. I was talking about Sand and Kay. It ain't no biggie."

Champ looked at his friend and started laughing, "Yeah! Fuck that shit. Fire up the weed, man!"

He lit it up and as they were getting high, he said, "So you've been hanging out with Corey old goofy ass, huh?"

"Yeah, man," Champ pulled on the reefer and passed it back to him.

Champ didn't know who was worse, Busty or Bruce. They got in a few more laughs before Busty said, "I bet you didn't know that Bruce fat ass had that bitch Lynn at the crib last night waxing that ass?"

"That don't surprise me wit' his nasty ass," Champ said, and they started laughing again. Busty took a puff off the reefer and passed it to him. That's when Champ asked, "Man, what is up with that bitch on the cheerleading squad?"

"Which one?" he asked.

"LaToya Winnsboro," Champ said.

"That stuck up bitch?" Busty shouted. "That ho' wouldn't give me or Donkey any act right."

"Oh, yeah? Well, I think I can get her," Champ took another hit.

"You probably can if that nigga Jay wasn't tricking that bitch," Busty said.

"Who the fuck is Jay?" he asked as he passed the reefer back to Busty.

"He play wide receiver for the team," he said.

Champ asked, "What makes you think he a trick?"

"Man, every bitch in Cohen be talking 'bout how they want a football player because them niggas are sugar daddies."

"Oh, yeah? Sugar daddies, huh?" Champ smiled.

Even after all Busty told him about the football team, Champ still wanted LaToya and was going to get her.

About seven o'clock that night he talked to Silk in his office. He told Champ that his mom had called to talk to him and left a message with Silk to tell him that it was urgent, and that he gets back in touch with her as soon as possible.

Champ hopped in his car and headed across to Algiers. When he got to his mom's house, she told him that Pops had something very important that he wanted to talk to Champs about. He asked her, "What is this about?"

Moms replied, "All he said was to have you here at ten o'clock when he calls."

Champ chilled out and talked with Moms for an hour or so. She was telling him that his Aunt Mert was going to have a family reunion in about a month or so, and she wanted to bring Bo with them. She had learned to accept Champ's daddy's son after a while. At ten o'clock, Pops called and Champ answered the phone with, "Hey Pops! How are you doing up in there, man? Me and Bo gon' drop five C-notes in the mail tomorrow."

"Alright, but I didn't call to talk to you about that," he said.

Little did Champ know that his Mom had walked to the back of the house and picked up the phone to listen to their conversation. His father asked him to take care of some serious business that he couldn't do himself because he was incarcerated.

"B-b-but Pops?" Champ said, worried.

"No buts, Champ. Just do it!" he yelled. "And don't come and see me until it's done!" Then he hung up the phone.

Champ still had the phone to his ear and was in a daze. Then he put it down slowly as he thought about what Pops wanted him to do. He got up from off the sofa and yelled, "Momma, I am about to go!"

As he looked toward the room where his mom was, he could sense that she had been standing in the doorway of the living room watching for a few minutes. She said, "I thought you were coming to spend some time with your Momma? You know I brought home a fresh-baked Dutch chocolate cake from the bakery today."

He had a feeling that she was trying to keep him there for a reason. "It sounds delicious Ma, but I gotta run over to the post office and express Pops some money," as he stepped toward the door. "He been gambling again," but she knew better.

If anybody could tell when someone was lying, it was her. No one could ever look her in the face when lying. If they did, she would know. She said, "He so crazy. He went through all that to tell you he needed money, huh?"

Champ opened the door and said, "Maybe one day he will learn to appreciate it," and he left. After he left the house, Champ's momma stared at the door and the wells of her eyes began to fill up with tears. She was thinking about what she overheard on the phone, and then the tears started coming down even more.

At the car wash, Bo and Champ were sitting in Bo's Eldorado, which was parked under the third cover. Bo yelled, "What the fuck you mean, take care of it?" as he pounded on the steering wheel.

"What the fuck are you tripping on?" his brother replied, "All he said was to do it, and don't come see him until it's done." Champ was calmer about the situation than Bo.

They sat in the Eldorado in silence for a while. Bo finally started the car and said, "Alright, we just gon' do it and get it over with, and just fuck it!" He put the car in drive. "I can't believe this shit," he said as they pulled out of the car wash.

Champ's mother was sitting in the front room watching an episode of Barnaby Jones at the time. She started thinking about what she had heard on the phone: "I want you to kill him, Champ." She rushed from the living room to the bedroom, picked up the phone, and began to dial a number. At the same time, Bo and Champ had pulled up in front of the house where she was calling.

Champ got out, pulled a ski mask over his face, and popped a bullet into the chamber of the .45. Bo put his mask on and spun the barrel on the .357 magnum, which was fully loaded. He then said, "Stay behind me" and hopped out of the car.

They got out and both walked toward the house. Champ said, "What the fuck you mean stay behind you?"

Bo replied "Cause I'm the oldest, Champ."

"Twenty-two days! So what!" he said under his breath.

Inside the house, their pop's best friend Leroy had awakened from his sleep to answer the phone. He looked at the clock on the nightstand. It read 11:30 PM. On the other end of the phone, their mother was mumbling to herself, "Wake up, Leroy, wake up," as the phone continued to ring.

Leroy picked up the phone and said, "Hello?"

She yelled, "Leroy! Leroy! Listen to me!"

"Yeah Debra, I'm listening!" he said.

"Leroy, you gotta get outta there!"

"What you talking 'bout?" He asked, and then he heard a knock at the front door. "Hold up, somebody is knocking at the door."

"Don't answer the door, Leroy! Don't answer it!"

Leroy ignored her and said, "Hold on a minute." He dropped the phone on the bed. He glanced at the clock and mumbled, "It's eleven-mutha-fuckin'-thirty-two, and who the fuck is this?" as he grabbed the knob on the door.

As she listened on the phone, she heard somebody yell, "Back up, mutha fucka!" and the tears began to roll down her face as she listened.

Bo shoved Leroy into the house and onto the floor. Champ ran through the house to make sure that there was no one else there. As he got to the back and started back up to the front, Champ heard six shots being fired. When he made it to the front, Bo said, "Let's get the fuck out of here!"

That's when Champ noticed that the phone was off the hook. He picked up the phone and said, "Hello! Hello!" He didn't know that his mom was on the other end crying in silence, as she heard her son's voice. Champ said, "There ain't nobody there," and then he hung up the phone.

They got in the car and left. His momma was left crying her eyes out. She and Leroy had been private lovers for years, and her husband had just found out.

CHAPTER SIX

The next day was Tuesday, and even though they had killed a man who was just like family, it really didn't bother them at all. Once Pops had given the word, he meant nothing to them at all. Champ was in the cafeteria getting his grub on with Corey and Isaac, as usual. Most of the fellas with cars or trucks would leave the grounds at lunchtime, but he tried to appear as normal as possible. He stood out in every crowd and hated it, because Big Bruce and the rest of the gang made it very hard for him not to get noticed.

While Champ was eating, Corey said, "Say, bro. After school we can cruise around Xavier Prep while the cheerleaders is practicing."

Champ thought about Kay, and said, "Cool."

Isaac said, "The team is going to practice and shit." That's when two guys walked up and asked Isaac if he was going to practice today. Isaac nodded his head yes and the guys replied, "Alright, cool." And just like that, they walked off.

Champ looked at Isaac and said, "You gotta do what you gotta do."

Just then, Corey mumbled, "Ah, shit!" Champ looked behind him and saw the nigga from the schoolyard and three more fellas. As they approached them, Champ stood up and prepared to defend himself. There wasn't anyone holding them back as they got in striking distance. They both ran into a tussle. The cafeteria got out of control as everybody rushed over to see Champ and a guy named Jay, go blow for blow. They came out of a mix and back into another one. It was just like the gang to be checking off the grounds during this time. He grabbed hold of Champ, making it difficult to swing at him. He attempted to push

Champ to the ground, but he held on to him. Then they both went crashing into the garbage can. He wouldn't let Champ go, and vice versa. Then the security guards at the school grabbed both of them and broke it up. Jay shouted, "Mutha Fucka, it ain't over yet! It ain't over!"

But Champ? He was calm, cool, and collected. The only damage done to him was a small hickey on the left side of his eye and a busted lip, but he had blood everywhere. One of the guards yelled, "Everybody get to your classes!" The bell for the fourth period class started ringing, and they were escorted to the office.

In the principal's office, Jay sat in one chair and Champ sat in another. Principal Hanes said to him, "Jason, look, this is your third quarrel in two weeks. Wha'cha think I ought to do?"

Jason looked at Mr. Hanes and replied, "Just one more chance, Mr. Hanes. I promise you I won't give you any more problems."

Mr. Hanes looked at him for a while, as if feeling sorry for him. Finally, Mr. Hanes asked, "You know what? Your coach and I talked to your Daddy about this. No top university will want you if you can't control your attitude," he picked up a pen and started writing on a piece of paper. "Whose class are you in?"

"Mrs. Randall's class, Sir," and he handed him a pass. "You go let the nurse fix you up. And Jason," he hesitated "the well's going dry." Jason nodded and left the office.

Mr. Hanes then turned to Champ and said, "Now, what did you say your name was?"

"Wayne Randolph," he replied. He reached into his desk drawer for some paperwork while saying, "Okay, Wayne. I'm going to have you bring in your parents tomorrow morning before nine o'clock," as he continued to write on some paper.

A frown formed on Champ's face instantly and he asked, "What you writing me up for?"

"It's the policy," Principal Hanes replied.

"Policy, shit! You ain't writing that nigga up!"

"You gon' watch your language in this office, ya hear?" he replied as he looked straight into Champ's eyes.

Champ just stared right back at him and he continued by saying, "I have been in the school system for twenty-three years, and I have seen them come and go. Some good and some bad, but I have had respect for them all." Champ knew then that he had pissed him off. "I don't know which one of them projects ya' come from; Calliope, St. Thomas, Third Ward, or the Tenth Ward," as he pointed his finger at him, "but the students at Cohen are represented by me. So if you come to Walter L. Cohen, you in B.R. Hanes's ward. You got that?" He looked Champ in his eyes hard this time.

Then he replied, "Yeah, I got it!"

"Oh! The reason why I want to see your parents is because you are a new student and I like to talk to the parents to let them know what I do and what I don't tolerate here." He then picked up some paper and rested back in his chair. He continued, "So you went to Fotier last year, huh?"

"Yeah."

"My good friend Mr. Brown is the principal over there in Pigeon Town. Did you give him any problems while you were over there?" he asked.

"We met," Champ answered vaguely on purpose.

He placed the papers back on his desk and said, "Now listen to me, Wayne. Me and this school can be anything you want it to be" He held up his left hand, "I can be your friend and we share some good times," he held up his right hand "or I can be your worst enemy and make your life fucked up. Now you choose." He turned around in his chair like Silk use to do and said, "Now good day, Mr. Randolph."

After he left Mr. Hanes's office, Champ went to his fourth period class. Ms. Baker, his Algebra II teacher, gave him his assignment since he wasn't there at the beginning of the class. The whole class had heard about the fight and was staring at him. He went back to his desk and started his work.

Then the strangest thing happened. Mr. Hanes barged into the classroom and said, "Excuse me." He looked toward the back of the class and spotted Champ, saying, "I'm checking you out. Get up and come with me."

Champ just looked at him. *What the hell*, he thought. The entire class looked at him. He had the limelight, if he ever saw it. Mr. Hanes looked at Champ with this sneaky grin on his face and said, "From now on, you rolling with the Hanes Gang. Ask around, somebody will tell you about me."

Then he looked at Ms. Baker and said, "If he gives you any problems just call me and I will ship his tail back to Pigeon Town." The whole class started laughing. As Hanes walked out of the classroom he peeped back at Champ and said, "You are hotter than the gun that killed Kennedy right now, aren't you?" and then he left the room.

School ended, and Champ headed around to Mrs. Well's class (she taught Biology). Corey was staying late to get extra help. It was hard for him to pass, and he wanted finish it. When Champ arrived at the classroom, Corey was seated in the third row, two seats from the back. Champ tried to get his attention by whispering, "Psssst. Psssst."

He finally looked out the door at Champ and gave him a "five minutes" hand signal. Champ waited, but something like twelve minutes had passed when he came out. "Nigga, you taking a long time and shit," he said.

They started walking down the hall on their way outside. He said, "Man that shit too fucking complicated."

Champ started laughing, "Naw, nigga. Your ass is just

plain dumb!"

"Aw, fuck you, nigga!" he replied. They both laughed again.

At the end of the hall, they came to a corridor that led into another hall, which lead out to the schoolyard. As Corey opened the door, he turned around and said, "Oh, yeah. Mutha fucka, when it's time to graduate, as long as I have my twenty-three credits, I'm cool."

As they both pushed the swing door open, they saw something black coming over their heads and Corey yelled, "What the fuck is going on?"

"Hey, mutha fucka!" Champ yelled and then something or someone struck him across the head and he was knocked unconscious.

When Champ came to, he was lying face down on the floor of the bathroom in a puddle of blood. It was hard for him to open his eyes. He felt a tremendous, vicious pain in his head. The first thing that he moved was his fingers. Upon doing so, he thought to himself, *At least I can move something.* Next, he tried to get up. Then he felt an awful, devastating pain in his left arm. He couldn't get it to budge. It became obvious to him that it was broken.

Then Champ rolled his body over onto his right side, so he could lie on his back. He turned his head slowly to look in the other direction and that's when he noticed Corey. Corey was lying on his back in a puddle of blood, about five feet away from Champ. He tried calling out his name as loudly as possible, "Corey! Corey!" But Corey never said a word, nor did he move.

Champ figured that Corey was hurt very badly and that the situation was grim. He knew that he had to help him. He leaned over to his right and slowly lifted himself up with his right arm. Feeling what seemed like endless, fierce pain, he brought himself to his feet. That is when he noticed that his pockets were turned inside out and everything that he had in them was scattered all over the bathroom floor, except his money. Champ staggered over to Corey and kicked him on his leg, trying to wake him by saying, "Wake up, nigga." Champ said it again, but he wouldn't wake up.

He knew then that Corey was hurt bad. He figured that he could get him to his car and take him to the hospital. Champ grabbed him by his shirt collar and tried to pull him to the door, but he was too heavy. And Champ was too weak. On top of that, he had a broken arm. He told Corey that he would be back, and he staggered out into the hallway.

The bathroom was on the base floor so all Champ had to do was walk two halls to the schoolyard. He walked down one hallway and came to a corridor which led to another. As he was going through the corridor, he heard someone talking some distance away. He walked over into the hall and saw Mr. Hanes, the principal, talking to a guy who looked like a fireman. As Champ stood in the hallway, he heard Mr. Hanes yell, "I don't know who started the fire. Maybe an outsider."

As he finished his sentence, Mr. Hanes looked down the hallway and saw Champ leaning on the wall, his clothes covered with blood. "Oh, my God!" Mr. Hanes cried aloud to the firemen while running over to help Champ, "Get an ambulance over here, now!"

When he had reached Champ, he fell into his arms and the first thing that he asked him was, "Was that your Eldorado parked outside?"

He looked at him and said, "Wha'cha mean, was?"

He replied, "Was...as in, past tense. It's all burned up!"

Champ then stuttered, "C-C-Corey."

"Corey what?" asked Mr. Hanes.

He continued, "Bernard."

Mr. Hanes was very concerned. He asked, "Corey Bernard? What about him, Wayne?"

He took a deep, shaky breath and then replied, "In the boy's bathroom," before he passed out again.

Champ woke up two days later. He was in the New Orleans Charity Hospital Intensive Care Unit, with his left arm in a cast. He had bandages wrapped around his rib cage and around his head as well. The first thing that he noticed was the television set on the wall. An old clipping of *Laurel and Hardy* that he and Bo used to watch at Ms. Katt's house was playing. An attempt to laugh was spoiled by an enormous pain in his head. He looked toward the window, and to his surprise, there was Sand cuddled up in a chair next to his bed, fast asleep.

"Wake up, sleepyhead," Champ said.

Sand opened her eyes and looked at him, then jumped out of her seat, full of joy. She ran over to his bed and gave him a long, passionate kiss, careful not to hurt him. She was glad that he had finally come through, and then she grabbed the telephone and started dialing. He asked, "What you doing?"

"Busty told me to call the shop whenever you come to," she replied.

After she made the call to the shop, Champ asked her, "Where's Corey?"

Sand's face turned serious. She answered him slowly, "They got him hooked up to all these machines and stuff. Champ, he's in a coma." Corey had been injured way worse than Champ. He was in the Critical Care Unit, fighting for his life.

"You been here with me all this time?" he asked Sand.

"Yeah, cause I thought you needed a Lil' tender, loving care," she replied.

Champ looked at her for a few seconds before asking, "What do you know about love?"

"Not much. But I do know that I love you!" she admitted.

He looked at her, astounded, thinking *Sand really loves me*. Then she said, "And you could have just asked me for some instead of doing what you did."

He looked at her with a curious look, thinking to himself, *I know Bianca ain't told her about me and her having sex*. Then Sand burst his bubble by adding, "Did you think Bianca wasn't going to tell me?"

Champ really looked and felt stupid. He then asked, "Tell you what?"

"About you telling Kay that you wanted to fuck her."

Whew! He was relieved. He took a deep breath and then asked, "How did you find out about that?"

Sand was quick to answer, "Bianca, dummy!" Champ started laughing lightly, but it wasn't at what she had said. He was thinking about how scandalous Bianca was.

She continued, "You know Minnie gon' tell Bianca everything."

"Yeah, well I thought it was about that time, but I didn't want to ask you," he stated.

Sand smacked her lips then asked, "So when she told you no, where you went?"

Now he was stuck. What was he gon' tell her? He couldn't tell her that he had sex before, and with her best friend at that. There would be a good chance of losing her for good. He just looked at her and said, "I just been taking my time to do everything ever since you have known me. I just got a little impatient and once she told me no I figured maybe it wasn't meant to be." He turned to look at the television and continued saying, "Besides, everything comes to those who wait." Neither of them said a word for a while. He was nervous as hell waiting. Champ didn't know if she was staring at him or not. He wasn't paying attention to what was on. He continued looking at the television.

Sand finally spoke and said, "You know what? Maybe you

won't be waiting as long as you think."

Sand and Champ were at his house one day after he was released from the hospital. It was a quarter to eleven, and Silk was giving the gang a birthday party. The party was going to start at two o'clock. It really was Dusty's birthday, which was on November 20[th.] Silk said that this party was the start of the gang's birthday season because Dusty, Bo, Redd, and Donkey's son Lil' Herman were born in November. Busty, Silk and Donkey's birthdays were in December. Big Bruce, Redd's girl Sunshine, Bianca, Minnie, the Fruit Man, Charlie the Barber, and I all had January birthdays.

Champ couldn't stop thinking and worrying about Corey. In fact, the tone was a bit subdued for everyone, even though he felt like trying to lighten things up.

The party started at two o'clock at Redd's house. Champ figured he'd hop in the tub a few minutes early so that he could have enough time to wrap his rib cage. He was sitting in a tub of nice warm water with the suds up to his chin, his left arm with the cast hanging outside of the tub, a reefer in his other hand, and a pillow behind his head for comfort. He was chilling and Sand yelled so that her voice could be heard over the Al Green album that was playing on the stereo in the living room, "You ain't drowned up in there, huh?"

Champ said loudly, "I'll be out in a minute."

"You know the party starts at two!"

"We gon' make it!" he replied, as he took a pull off the reefer and then started humming the tune of one of the songs on the album, "Love can make you do wrong, make you do right."

The bathroom door opened just a little, slowly. Champ took another pull off the reefer while looking in that direction. The door opened some more and Sand was standing in the doorway, naked as a newborn baby. He looked her up and down. He noticed that there wasn't a mark on her body. Her thighs were perfect. She had a small waistline and her nipples, hard and round, were just right. She was so beautiful. She walked over to the tub and placed one of her legs into the tub. Champ held her hand as she put her other leg into the tub.

Sand stood over Champ, naked, with fire burning in her eyes. He put the reefer out and put his hand on her calves. He slowly ran his hands up her thighs and placed them on the brown, fuzzy bush that blessed her pussy. He envied that fuzzy bush. He teased her by rubbing the lips of her clit softly with his index finger, and she purred like a cat. She was ready and she didn't have to tell him, because her body told him.

Cum ran down Champ's fingers to his knuckles. She was dripping wet already. He placed his hand on her waist, while he lowered her body down slowly. She was looking at him with love in her eyes and his dick stood straight up. She grabbed it with a firm grip and positioned it. She started lowering herself onto him, but it wouldn't go in. He looked at her, wondering what she wanted to do. She then placed both of her hands on both sides of the tub, while looking down at him. Her long, sandy hair flopped down in his face. She lowered herself onto his dick with a little more force, and she let out a loud scream as it went in.

She was in pain, as Champ's dick entered her virgin pussy, but she kept going. He was in heaven as he felt her walls close in on his dick. "Oh, Lord! Oooh! It's in my stomach!" she screamed as she came all the way down on his cock. She placed her hands on his chest and started going up and down at a nice, slow pace. She moaned and moaned, "Ooooh! Ooooh," every time she came down on it. Champ eased himself into her slowly, because he wanted to take advantage of her newly removed virgin hood. To be honest, he wanted to leave a mark behind. It was as if he didn't want her to leave, and like he was in love.

Then she stopped, stood up, got out of the tub, and told him to come on. He watched as she walked to the center of the bathroom, lay down on her back, and opened her legs wide. He could see the pinkness of her inner self. He got out of the tub and walked over to her. He dropped down to his knees, and lay down on top of her carefully, so that he didn't hurt his arm. She reached for his dick and put it inside of her. He put his good arm under her neck and the arm with the cast lied beside her head. He started doing his thing. From his experience with Bianca, he knew exactly how they wanted it. Champ eased in and out, in and out, and every so many strides he would thrust into her with a Lil' tap behind it, sort of ruthless. She placed her hands on his ass and pulled him deeper and deeper inside of her, as she nibbled on his left earlobe with her mouth. They kept up this pace for a little while. It felt so good to be inside her wet pussy. She was into it and then she started crying out to me, "Don't leave me no more, Champ! Please! Don't leave me!"

The pace started building up a bit and her pussy was feeling more like heaven. The slow pace turned into a passionate, feverish rhythm. Suddenly, she called out, "Champ! Oooh, Baby! Ba-by, I love you!"

Champ was about to cum, but he didn't want to just yet because it had only been thirty-two minutes. He wanted it to be as if it was when he had sex with Bianca, so he stopped. Sand was inhaling deeply, as he lifted himself off her she asked, "You come yet?"

"Naw," he said, and stood up.

She noticed that his cock was still erect so she asked, "Then what's wrong?"

Champ grabbed a towel, wrapped it around his waist and walked into the bedroom. She got up, and put a towel around her body. She came into the bedroom behind him.

Once they were in the room, he realized that she was pissed off because he had not cum inside of her.

"So why didn't you finish?" she asked, confused.

Champ walked over to his dresser, picked up some a deodorant stick, and said, "I was about to cum."

"So what happened?"

"Not in thirty-minutes," he replied.

She folded her arms, leaned on the door and replied, "Donkey and Bianca stretched twenty-five minutes. I would say that you did pretty well for the first time." He turned and looked at her, surprised at what she had just said. "Halloween night, what did you stretch? An hour and forty-five minutes?" she asked.

Champ continued to just stare at her. She had this sassy look on her face, and she would not back off. So he said, "Bianca tells you everything, huh?"

"Donkey tells you everything. Right?" she retorted.

Champ started laughing, and she started blushing. "So what you really trying to tell me is, whenever I do my thing, do it right, huh?"

She replied, "Ain't that what you trying to tell me?"

She walked up behind him and wrapped her arms around his waist, as he groomed himself in the mirror. He said, "I don't tell Donkey everything." He then turned around and pulled her closer to him, rested both of his hands on her ass and gave her a long, passionate kiss. Champ thought to himself, *If either of us are hiding something* (and he knew that he was), *then we both have real excuses to know what we were doing.*

At one o'clock, Champ and Sand were both dressed and on their way to the party. From Champ's house in Kenner, to Redd's new house in New Orleans East, it took about thirty minutes driving time. It was one-thirty when they arrived, and there was a great group of people already there. Champ was stopped by Dusty as soon as he entered the door. He walked up and said, "Man, you just missed everybody."

"Where they went?" Champ asked. *Why did I just ask that?* He thought to himself. Then Dusty gave him a whole, long-ass story.

"Ain't nobody here but me, your mom, Silk, and a few of Silk's and Redd's friends. Donkey and Bianca are gone uptown to pick up of some friends. Bruce took them in his car because it's a lot of girls. Busty is gone to pick up my cousin Herman. They gon' bring a few hoes from out of the Seventeenth Ward for Donkey." Nine times out of ten, Donkey was coming over here in a hot car. None of them wanted to see him go to jail.

Dusty continued, "They gon' stop at one of the stores and get some more chips and shit for the party. Bo gon' pick up Reggie and a few hoes off the cheerleading squad at y'all school, and on his way back he gon' shoot over to St. Thomas Projects and pick up your podna, Isaac."

Champ just looked at him first. He simply wanted to see if Dusty's ass was outta breath after spewing out all of those words. Then he said, "Yeah? Well, that's cool." Then he walked over to the couch and took a seat. "Where did Redd go?"

Dusty looked at him as if he were surprised and replied, "Huh?"

Champ looked at him briefly, wondering why he was looking at me like that. Then he asked again, "Redd? Where he at?"

"Oh! Redd had to go take care of some business for Silk. He'll be back in a few minutes." He looked at Dusty curiously, because he was acting very strange. Champ glanced over at Sand and realized she was acting weird, too. He turned back to Dusty and said, "You got one of them Lil' hoes up in here, huh?"

He put his index finger on his lips and said, "Sshhh!"

Sand looked at Champ and said, "You know he picked all that up from y'all." Champ started laughing.

Then Sunshine walked in and said, "Oh, y'all finally made it, huh?" She looked around and said, "Them mutha fuckas better stay their asses right in that backyard or in that garage cause they ain't gon' sit all over my shit!"

Sand replied, "I'm telling ya!"

At about one fifty-five, everybody started coming in. Donkey, Bianca, and Minnie walked in with about eight or nine of their girlfriends from school. Bruce was right behind them. Busty showed up with Donkey's cousin, Herman, and three broads that Champ went to Fortier with the previous year. One of them was Angie. She was the captain of the Flag Twirlers. He tried to get a conversation out of her once. She told him that she was faithful to her boyfriend, so he had left it alone. Kissing ass was never Champ's style, even though her boyfriend was locked up.

Bo showed up with Reggie Jones, Isaac, and about four of the cheerleaders from Cohen. The look that Minnie gave him was priceless. A few people who were not from the neighborhood came, plus a kid named Robbie who lived on the next block. He was sweet on Sand when she first moved around there. He ended up being friends with Redd. Redd liked him because he had a little experience in the heroin world, and he always came with raggedy money. Redd said that raggedy money always caught his eyes in a hustler. Then there was Champ's brother-in-law Mark, and Reuben, who was his older brother. Reuben was Holly's baby daddy. He didn't stay far away, and he had brought a few broads with him.

Once the party started, everyone was dancing and having a good time. Reefer smoke was everywhere and people were drinking, too. All of a sudden, the music stopped and everyone looked at the DJ, only to see Redd standing next to him. Champ leaned back onto the garage door, turned to Busty and said, "I wonder what he is up to?" as he handed the reefer to him.

He handed it back and replied, "Man, you just never know."

Redd said, "I know y'all want to continue getting yawl's groove on, but I just stepped in and want to wish the boys a Happy Birthday!" He held up a glass of Remy Martin in the air indicating a toast, and yelled, "Happy Birthday, Fellas!"

The gang held up their hands. Someone in the background asked, "Are all these birthdays on the same day?" Everybody laughed.

Then the garage door started moving, "Man what the fuck?" Busty and Champ stepped away from the garage door, and then Redd said, "Happy Birthday, Champ!"

As everybody stared into the garage, Champ's eyes suddenly opened up real wide. He was staring at a shiny, stunning, chocolate brown, brand-new Eldorado. It had a peanut butter-colored leather interior with matching vinyl top, chrome and gold grill, gold Dayton rims, Vogue tires, and dope sound. She was a beauty. Since Champ's old Eldorado was destroyed, Redd and Silk had put together and bought him another one. This one was even more exceptional than the first one. Champ was very grateful and loved it.

When it was time to leave the party, everybody left with whom they had come with except Isaac. Champ told him to ride with him instead of Bo. It was something that he wanted to do. He had a brand-new Eldorado, his girl sitting next to him, and his dog in the back seat.

Bo was letting Reggie into the back seat of his car. Minnie, who insisted on riding with him, was letting two girls in the back from the other side. Bo said, "Lil' brother, you gon' be alright?"

Champ looked over at him and they both smiled. He always insisted on being the oldest. Bo got into his car. Champ tried to open his new car's door but couldn't, due to his arm being in a cast. Bo pulled off, and Sand looked at Champ. She noticed that he was having problems opening his door so she said, "Bae, you want me to drive?"

He looked at her. She knew exactly what was on his mind, so she said, "I'm always pushing my daddy's Fleetwood, and so you know I can handle an Eldorado."

He looked at Isaac, and he hunched his shoulders as if saying, *I ain't in that*. Champ looked back at Sand, stared at her for a bit, and then said, "Alright; you drive."

When they made it to Isaac's house, Champ opened the door to let him out while asking, "Wha'cha doing tomorrow?"

He stepped out of the car, gave me a firm handshake, and replied, "I'ma sleep until noon and then my cousin is gon' pick me up to go shoot some baskets at Kingsley's house."

"Alright then. I'ma see you at school Monday," Champ replied.

Isaac smiled. "Later," he replied, and then they left.

After dropping him off, Champ and Sand were heading to his house. Sand leaned over, ejected his Marvin Gaye tape, and slipped another tape in. It was Sade. She said that she listened to it whenever her daddy let her drive his Fleetwood. She hit the interstate and started heading west as they listened to the smooth sound of a song called *Is It a Crime?* They rode on the interstate and approached the exit leading to Champ's house. Just as Sand drove down the ramp to a red light a few blocks away from his house, Champ turned around and said, "Turn around and get back on the interstate."

"What?" she questioned him, surprised.

"I want you to get back on the Interstate!" he spoke with

authority.

"Right. Whatever you say, Boss!" she said sarcastically, as she made a U-turn around the neutral and then got back on the interstate. She was wondering what he was up to. Every now and then she'd glance over at Champ as he stared out the window looking like he didn't want to be bothered.

They approached the Elysian Fields exit and he said," Get off here." She looked at him, and then exited off the interstate.

"Let me know when you want me to turn," she said.

"You gon' know!" he replied, still aggravated.

As they rode down Elysian Fields Avenue, they came to a stop sign at Lake Shore Drive. After stopping the car, she asked, "Which way?"

"Right," Champ answered.

She made the right turn and headed down Lake Shore Drive. An eight-block stretch ran along the lake. The lake was a lovely sight at night. The sound of the waves smashing against the concrete steps was usually the only thing a person heard, unless there was somebody out there cranking up their music. As they neared the middle of the stretch, he told her to pick a spot and park.

They rode for a little distance and she parked by an area where a dim light strained through a group of oak trees. She put the car in park and then turned off the ignition off. Just then, a patrolman passed by and shined a spotlight through the rear-view window. He saw nothing strange or suspicious, so he cruised on by. Sand looked at Champ and asked, "So why we stopping here?"

He snatched her by the neck, sort of ruthless and with a slightly tight squeeze. She looked at him like he was crazy and then he said, "I gotta do it right, remember?"

She inhaled sharply as Champ pressed her lips against his. She quickly started to like this game, came across the seat, and sat on top of him. He pulled her short jean mini-skirt up and placed his hand inside her panties to grip her ass. She started unbuckling his pants. Then she eased her hand into his pants to pull out his cock. She grabbed it and started massaging it. He pulled her panties to one side and slid his throbbing dick inside her wet pussy. When it was all the way inside of her, she wrapped her arms around his neck and started riding him up and down, up and down. She rode him for every bit of about forty-five minutes.

At Donkey's house, Bianca was leaning forward, over the dresser while he stood behind her, stabbing his cock inside of her again and again, as she screamed out, "Oh Donk-Donkey baby, please!" She was in pain, but loved every bit of it. Her nipples were hard and erect. Sweat ran down both of their bodies. Donkey was pumping his dick into her in a very ruthless and rapid manner as she continued to scream louder and louder, until she woke up her son Lil' Herman. He had been asleep in the other room.

At Bo's house there was also something going on. He was lying on top of Minnie with her right leg propped up on his shoulders. Her left leg was cuffed under his arm and he was at a slow, lovemaking pace. His slow strides sent chills through Minnie's spine. She closed her eyes, began to rub his back with one hand, and rubbed his ass with the other, as she let out moans of passion.

In the Carrolton Area, Busty had met this broad who had come to the party with Donkey's cousin Herman, named Tracey. She had insisted on going to her house that night instead of his. They ended up having sex on the back porch at her house on a washing machine. His jeans were dropped down to his knees and she wrapped her legs around his waist. He thrust into her while gripping her ass tightly to keep her steady. She put one of her hands over her mouth to keep the screams of pain from bursting out. The dogs were barking from the other yard as the washing machine rocked on the wooden porch, making this annoying sound.

At Bruce's house, he and Dusty sat beside each other on the living room couch. Bruce looked at Dusty and said, "That new Eldog's a beauty, huh?"

"Fucking right!" Dusty agreed. "Man, did you see those rims?"

"See them?" Bruce shouted, "Nigga! I went with Redd to get the mutha fuckas."

"Man, I can't wait until we find out who did that to him. That nigga know who did it," Dusty replied, "but for some reason he don't want to get into it right now. But you know? I think it was that nigga Jay." Dusty said.

"Ah, bitch! Yo' teeth hurt!" Bruce yelled out.

"I'm sorry, baby!" said the girl working on Bruce.

"Yeah, yeah, bitch! You just finish doing what you doing!" Bruce replied as he rested his head back on the sofa. "Dusty, how are you doing over there?"

"Ah, nigga! It's cool." He rested back on the sofa as well. They were with two broads from Redd's neighborhood who were now on their knees sucking on their cocks. It wasn't something new. They did that kind of often.

The next day at Jane Lee's beauty salon, Kay asked her stepmom if anyone had called for her while she was sleeping. Janie Lee, who had Sand's head under a sink rinsing her hair replied, "Now Katie, you know I be too busy on a Sunday to mess with that phone. Go ask yo' Nana."

Glo walked in the room and said, "Ask me what?"

Kay asked Glo, "Did anybody call for me?"

Glo walked over to Bianca who sat under the hair dryer, cut the hair dryer off and raised the lid from over her head.

"I have been up since nine and the only person that called was June."

"What he want?" asked Jane Lee.

"You know how his drunk ass gets when I don't give him none," and everybody started laughing.

Minnie had some hair styling skills of her own. Her momma had set up a beauty salon in the house that she was raised in fourteen years before. She sat in a chair looking in a mirror while hot curling her hair, looked at Sand and said, "Yeah, girl! Tell us about last night."

Bianca starting smiling and said, "Now ain't you nosey?"

"Baby, I'm nosey, too" giggled Jane Lee. "Now what happened last night?" she asked.

Not far away at Mr. Charlie's barbershop, the gang was there getting fresh haircuts. Mr. Charlie said to Bo, "Now you said you just want a little off the top?"

"Yeah!" said Bo.

Dusty said, "Bo, did you look at Double-O-Seven last night on cable?" as he sipped on a soda.

Bo replied, "Nigga, I wasn't worried about no James Bond. I was too busy being the mack that I am, if anything."

Busty mumbled, "Wanna-be mack," and everybody within earshot chuckled.

Back at the salon, as she put some shiny rollers into Bianca's hair, Glo yelled, "Every time I see one of them Lil' mutha fuckas, they be speaking to me like they so innocent, but I ain't think they was like that." She put her hands on her hips, "She-it! I couldn't get an hour and a half out of June if I got him piss-ass drunk."

"Aw Glo', shut up!" Jane Lee shouted. "June ass couldn't get up that long if y'all fucked in a liquor store!" Everyone in the beauty salon cracked up.

Jane Lee looked down at Sand and said, "What about you?"

Sand blushed, "Who? Me?"

"What the fuck are we running here? A salon? Or a pet shop? Cause you sure sounds like an owl to me." Sand laughed and then started telling them about last night.

At the barbershop, Bruce was talking smack, too. "Yeah! A mutha fucka think a nigga don't know 'bout him." At that point, everybody was curious, wondering who he was talking about. He looked at Champ and said, "Nigga, you know who I'm talking about."

"Who? Me?" Champ asked, looking at Bruce as if he was crazy.

"Yeah, nigga!" Dusty replied. "We know you and Sand is in love." They all started laughing.

Bruce said, "What's next? Marriage?"

"Nigga, my dog can't never be in love," Donkey said as he flipped through a magazine and continued. "Our mack is too strong."

"Yeah, nigga!" Champ replied as he gave Donkey a firm handshake.

At the salon, Jane Lee shouted, "On the lake! Which one is that?"

"Champ!" Minnie yelled. The whole salon got quiet and everybody stopped what he or she was doing.

Jane Lee looked at Kay and asked, "Well, ain't that Champ the one you was messing with?" Kay was speechless.

"I told you, Jane Lee!" Glo shouted. "That day that Lil' boy first came in here I knew he was gon' be a heartbreaker."

"More like broke his heart," Minnie said.

Jane Lee asked, "And how did she end up breaking his heart?"

Minnie continued doing her own hair and said, "Momma, do you think somebody gon' wait five years for some?"

"He did!" shouted Kay.

"And you ain't give it to him now he gone!" yelled Minnie. That's when the argument started.

"Shut up, goddammit!" replied Jane Lee, and looked at them both. "What I told y'all 'bout that shit in my house?" Then she asked, "Y'all sound like two Praydes Street hoes fussing about a nigga!"

"That don't belong to none of them!" Glo added.

Kay replied, "Yeah! But she always takes up for him."

"Cause you don't deserve him!" replied Minnie.

"Wait a minute!" yelled Jane Lee as she began to get angry, "Watch me knock you two hoes on y'all asses! Now I don't want to hear anymore. Y'all hear me?" She looked at them both with a frown on her face. Minnie and Kay nodded their heads. "Now Katie," she continued, "Go look in my closet and get a jar of setting gel."

As Kay turned to go toward the closet, she mumbled, "I can still get him back if I want." She had mumbled it loud enough for everyone to hear.

"Bitch, watch me smack the piss outta you!" Jane Lee said.

Later on that day Busty, Donkey and Champ were riding around in his Cadi, smoking a reefer, just chilling. The cars wouldn't start pulling in until about two o'clock on Sunday, so they let Bruce and Bo hold everything down since it was only eleven. They were going up Magnolia Street to Jackson Avenue, and as Champ took a left heading to Claiborne, Donkey said, "But for real, Champ! What we gon' do 'bout them niggas, brash?" As Champ brought the car to a halt at a red light, Donkey added, "It's obvious who did it."

Busty said, "For real."

Champ replied, "I'ma' handle it my way." As the light turned green, he made a left turn and headed down Claiborne toward Washington.

"Man, fuck all that! Let me kill about two of them niggas," Busty yelled.

"Two? Shit, it was more than that!" Donkey yelled.

"Well fuck it!" replied Busty, "Kill the whole team!" They both laughed.

Champ looked at them both as they laughed but didn't find anything funny, so he said, "That's what the fuck they want to see." He passed the reefer to Donkey.

He took a puff off it and then said, "Then we gon' give it to 'em." They started laughing again. Champ looked at them both once more, with an angry look on his face. They were laughing uncontrollably. Champ was getting progressively more annoyed with the two of them. He passed in front of a Winn Dixie Supermarket and came up to Toledano Street, pulled over to the curb, and yelled, "Get the fuck out!"

Donkey then said, "Man, we just fucking around."

He repeated himself, "Get the fuck out!"

Busty said, "Man, look at all these people looking at us!"

He did not look around, nor did he care. He yelled again, "I don't give a fuck. Get out!"

Donkey looked at Champ and said, "You serious?"

Champ replied, "You mutha fuckin' right!"

"Well fuck it, then!" Busty said. "We can walk."

And as Donkey opened the passenger door and they got out, he said to Champ, "But we still gon' kill the football team." They started laughing again.

After closing the door, Busty looked in Champ's window and said, "Two-thirty-two, hut, hut, hut!"

Then Donkey said, "Ratta-tat-tat on that ass!"

Champ said, "You nigga's stupid!" Then he pulled off. He saw them laughing in the rear-view mirror. He thought it was all a big joke to them. He was just riding around, thinking. He couldn't believe them, joking about killing a whole football team...but then he started laughing to himself. He pictured how that would look: twenty-three mutha fuckas wrapped in body bags. No way; he just couldn't see that.

Donkey rode around for about an hour, and eventually ended up back at the car wash. When he got out of his car, he started laughing. There was Busty standing in the middle of the lot in a three-point stance, with Donkey behind him acting like a quarterback. Busty ran out about ten yards yelling, "Here I go! Here I go!" Then Donkey pretended as if he had a gun and shot him down. Champ nodded his head while grinning, and then Busty ran over to him and said, "Now, Dog, on the real, your momma passed over here."

"What she want?" he asked, as they walked over to Donkey who was chilling in front of the office. "She just needed a few dollars and shit. So I gave her fifty dollars," he said.

"Cool. I'ma give it to ya'."

"Man, don't trip on that shit," said Busty, "cause you would give it to Mr. Ben."

We started horsing around and all of a sudden, we heard somebody yell, "Champ!" It was Sand, and she was with Minnie, Bianca, and a new broad that we had never seen before.

Donkey asked, "Man, who the fuck that is?"

As we walk over to them, Busty said, "Chill, Donkey. I got this!" And as soon as we got over to them, Busty called the new girl to the side and started putting his mack down.

Champ asked Sand, "What's up?"

"We are going to Winn Dixie for Jane Lee, and I come to see if you want anything." He really didn't want anything, but since she was asking, he told her to bring him a bag of Cheez-Whiz and a cold drink.

"What kind?" she asked?

"Root beer," he replied.

Bianca and Donkey was all hugged up and kissing, as usual. Sand grabbed her by the arm and said, "Y'all got a house. Y'all can do that in there."

As they walked away, Donkey shouted, "Girl! You better not pull on her no mo!" He had a real attitude in his tone, and Champ had to check that.

"Nigga! You better watch how you talk to her!" he warned Donkey.

"Fuck you, nigga!" he replied, and they started horsing around again.

Later on that day after the car wash had closed Champ shot across the river to his mom's for a Lil' while. It was really just one of those days where he and Bianca just shot the breeze. He would usually talk to her from Holly's house, but the gang started hanging out there the majority of the time. So he started using my mom's phone. Bianca asked, "Why you trying to hide your feelings for her?"

He stretched out on the couch and said, "I ain't hiding my feelings. I just don't love her."

"Oh! I understand. That's all in putting your mack down, huh? Like Donkey be saying," she said sarcastically, and Champ started laughing. Then she said, "You think I don't be knowing 'bout them hoes Donkey be fucking? As long as he takes care of me and my baby, I don't give a fuck!" Then she said, "What'd you do if one of them hoes got pregnant?" Champ got quiet and she felt his nerves. Then she asked, "What would you do if I got pregnant for you?"

He replied quickly, "Ma'am, I don't even want to think about that!"

"Alright then. Back to what we were talking 'bout. Why boys don't like to admit when they have feelings for a girl?" she asked.

He replied, "I ain't saying that I didn't have feelings for her."

"Then if you have feelings for her, why you don't show her?" Bianca asked him, straight up.

"I'm showing her now," he replied.

"How? By breaking her virginity and hanging around all the time? Because that ain't gon' even do it." Bianca laid it out. He supposed he needed to hear it.

Champ asked her, "What else a nigga 'sposed to do?"

"It's a lot of shit you can do," she replied.

"Like what?" he asked.

"You can start by buying her something," Bianca suggested.

"Shit, you can't name one thing that Sand don't have. Cause you know that she Redd's daughter."

Bianca was silent for a moment and then said, "I know something that she doesn't have."

He was very interested. "What?"

Bianca answered, "A car!"

Champ shouted out, "A car? Man, you must be crazy!"

"What, you embarrassed to let your boys know you bought your old lady a car?" she teased.

"It ain't that," he said, but he still had no reason.

"Then what is it?" she asked.

He couldn't have given her an answer if his life depended on it. He thought it was that commitment thing.

Champ had gotten home from the hospital and returned to school. He was wearing a money-green long sleeved silk shirt, a pair of black Levis, dark green Bally Hunters, and a black leather jacket that everyone had started to wear. He rode in his car with Sand by his side and Isaac sat in the back. Corey would've been with them, but he was still in a coma fighting for his life.

All eyes were on them as they pulled into the schoolyard. Sand and Champ were in front, and Bo was behind them with Minnie. Donkey rolled up with Bianca. Busty was alone, and so was Big Bruce. Everyone stared at the dark brown Eldorado with the fancy rims. It seemed as if the whole school was waiting on them to pull off a magic trick or something. It was impressive. They walked into the building looking like they were ready to rule the world.

As soon as they entered the building, they walked into the Principal, Mr. Hanes' office. He stopped them dead in their tracks and said, "I don't want any shit in my school, Wayne!"

He looked down at Champ's cast and asked, "Is that arm okay?"

He replied, "It's alright."

As the bell started ringing to begin the day, he said, "Come here and let me have a talk with you."

Bo said to Champ, "Check you later."

They walked to his office while he was yelling, telling everybody to get to class. He saw Big Bruce in the hall putting his mack down on a broad and he yelled, "Leonard! Get yo' heavy tail up to Ms. Jones' class, boy!" And Bruce rushed away.

When they got to his office, Mr. Hanes sat behind his desk and told Champ, "Take a seat. I want to tell you something." He sat down in a chair in front of his desk. Champ knew that he was going to talk to him about not bringing his parents with me. "Wayne, do you remember how long I told you that I have been in the school system?"

He said, "Mr. Hanes, my momma had to work!"

"I ain't worried about that."

Champ was unsure of his intentions and said, "So what do you want from me?"

Mr. Hanes looked at him and said, "On the first floor in front of Mr. Brady's class, you passed something to Benjamin Jackson, and he passed something to you by Derrick Sims and Bianca Cooks. Now, we both know what that was." He rested back in his seat. "I want you to go and bring it here, and I'll give it back to you after detention."

About thirty minutes later, Champ stepped into his office and sat a .45 caliber on top of his desk. He raised his head up to look at it. He had caught him in the middle of some paperwork. He then rested back in his chair and said, "Wayne, let me tell you something. On Friday past, there was a faculty meeting in the library." He started to fiddle with a fountain pen in his hand and continued, "We talked about the students cutting class, students coming to school high, students this, students that," and then he pointed at Champ. "Then there was a discussion on you."

"What y'all was talking about me for?" He put a frown on his face.

"Well. Some of the teachers are saying that you are a bad influence on the students here. That you intentionally encourage them to want to experience the fast life." He looked at the .45 on his desk and back at Champ, who just listened. "Then there were others who said that you were the aggressor in the fight with Jason Rodshu-"

Champ cut him off quickly, "That nigga started it!" He yelled.

"I know this, Wayne. But this is what I am trying to get you to understand. The teachers at Walter L. Cohen are saying you ain't gon' amount to shit!" He stood up from his chair. "They say you gon' be nothin' but a goddamn gangster!"

Right then, Champ started to think about what Big Head Simon had said about him a long time ago. Then Mr. Hanes continued, "That's why I took the gun from you. Because I'll prove every single one of them sons of bitches wrong, and goddammit if you ain't gon' help me!" He picked up a pen and started writing Champ a pass to class. He handed it to him and said, "Now. You get on up to Ms. Watkins's class." Champ nodded, looking him in the eyes. Then he started toward the door. "Oh, yeah. Tell Benjamin Jackson, Derrick

Sims, and Bianca Cooks to join you this afternoon for detention, ya' hear me?" added Mr. Hanes.

Champ replied, "Yeah! I hear ya. I do."

"Oh, and bring Bruce Leonard with ya for trying to distract me." Champ looked at him and smiled, then walked out the door.

Since Busty, Donkey, Big Bruce, and Champ were stuck in detention after school, Dusty and Bo were backed up at the car wash. Silk was making phone calls to a few houses in the neighborhood to people he knew with sons trying to get them some help, but he couldn't get any. Since it was only two of them, they decided to team up on each car to get it done faster. About a quarter to four, a navy blue Delta '88 pulled up just outside the car wash. Dusty, who was stooped down washing the rims of a Buick Park Avenue, glanced over at the car, and noticed that there were four men in it. They were looking directly over at Bo, who was washing the other side of the car. He had not noticed the four guys or the car. Dusty said in a calm way, while walking toward the office, "Heads up."

Bo looked up at him while saying, "What?" but he had already gone into the office.

Inside the office, Silk was still on the phone and Dusty yelled, "Gimme the gun!"

Silk leaned back, opened the drawer while still talking on the phone, and pulled out the Army .45. She handed it to Dusty. "I'ma pay the boy Maggie, just send him around here," Silk said to someone over the phone, as Dusty headed for the door with the .45 in his hand.

Outside the office, Bo had started back to washing the car when he heard someone scream, "Get out of the way!"

His eyes widened as he looked to see what the commotion was. He dropped the soap sponge, kicked over the bucket and began to run after seeing three masked men running toward him. Two of them had assault rifles and the other one had a shotgun. Everybody started to scatter when the first gun went off. The bullets missed Bo by inches, hitting a car as he ran past. Silk suddenly realized that Dusty had come and asked for his gun, and he had given it to him.

Dusty stepped out of the office and was within about ten or fifteen feet away from one of the gunmen. The gunman had an assault rifle. Without hesitation, Dusty aimed the .45 and started shooting. The gunman tumbled helplessly after he caught a bullet to his head, two in his neck, and one which made a side entry to his chest.

After watching him drop, Dusty turned to shoot the second gunman. The gunman was aiming right at him. They both pulled the trigger at the same time. The blast from the gunman's gun hit Dusty in his chest and slammed him into a Ford Bronco truck. He then fell to the ground, unconscious. The bullet from the .45 hit the gunmen in the neck and he fell to his knees while yelling, "Dee, I'm hit!"

The third gunman was running behind Bo, but heard as the other gunman yelled out to him. He went over to him and picked him up. They made their way to the waiting car as fast as they could. They got into their car and left. Silk rolled outside of the office and saw Dusty lying on the ground covered in blood and yelled, "Nooo!"

At the hospital, Busty, Bruce, Donkey, Bianca and Champ rushed into the emergency entrance. All of them were upset after learning of what had happened at the car wash. As soon as they walked in, they saw Bo and Silk. Donkey was totally out of control. He yelled, "Man! What the fuck happened to my Lil' brother?"

Silk yelled, "Donkey, calm down!"

"Man, fuck that!" Donkey yelled in anger.

"Donkey, chill out," Champ said as he noticed the doctor approaching. "Let's see what this man's talking about."

"Who's this kid's guardian?" They all pointed at Silk. "You his legal guardian?"

Silk replied, "Yeah."

"Okay," the doctor took a deep breath. "He has had some serious trauma."

"Fuck that!" yelled Donkey abruptly. "Is he gon' die?"

"He's not going to die, but you need to control yourself," the doctor said.

Bo shouted, "Donkey! Chill out!"

The doctor continued, "This being from a shotgun, the buck shots didn't penetrate his chest plate. So I assume that the gunmen were more than ten feet away or else he'd be dead. But that is not the problem at hand." He looked at all of them and said, "He is suffering from severe brain trauma and a fractured skull. He needs to undergo surgery right away."

Donkey broke down in tears. Bruce tried to comfort him, but he didn't want to talk to anyone. He walked over by the pay phone and cried. After the doctor left, Silk said, "Y'all look here. Y'all need to keep an eye on that boy, cause Donkey gon' do something stupid."

Just then, Busty said, "Damn! Where he at?"

We all ran to the doors and saw his Cadillac peeling out of the parking lot. Champ yelled, "Bianca, stay with Silk!" and then to the gang, "Come on! Let's find this nigga befo he do something stupid!" They all hopped in their cars and started looking for Donkey.

The first place Donkey went to was Nigger Town by his cousin Herman's house. Herman wasn't home, so he drove around certain areas where he thought he might be. Herman had a spot on Bernadette and Green Street where he would go and hide out whenever the law was rolling too hot, so he decided to go there. When he pulled up to the corner there were a few guys hanging out, so he rolled down his window and said, "Hey, y'all see my cousin Herman around here?"

One guy who recognized him yelled, "Herman just pulled off; he headed for the Olive Branch to pick up something."

"You know what he riding in?" Donkey asked.

"Yes! He's riding in Will's Cutlass!" the guy said.

Donkey pressed for more information, "The light blue one with the trues on it?"

The guy answered, "Yes." Donkey peeled off. The Olive Branch was a name given to the corner store in Holly Grove which wasn't far from Nigger Town, so Donkey hit Carrolton Avenue and headed straight there. As he came down Carrolton Avenue, he was stopped by a red light and got impatient. It seemed as if the light was taking forever to change, so he smashed down on the accelerator and ran it. He hit a left, headed toward Leonidas, and saw the light blue Cutlass that he was looking for. It was going in the opposite direction. He quickly switched from the outside lane to the inside lane and then made a left turn around the neutral ground, and started chasing after it. Herman was driving sort of fast as he made a right turn on Carrolton, but the Cutlass was no match for the Eldorado. Therefore, it was easy for Donkey to catch up with him. He honked his horn and flicked his high beams twice.

Herman thought to himself, 'What the fuck?' He looked in his rear view mirror and then said "Oh! That's Donk!" He rolled down his window and motioned for Donkey to follow him. Donkey followed Herman all the way back to Bernadette and Green Street. When Herman got out of his car, he had a small brown bag under his arm and a gun in the other hand.

They walked up to each other and Herman said, "Nigga, I'm rolling with a half a thang and a roscoe, so you know that I ain't stopping this mutha fucka 'til I get where I got to go," as they shook each other's hands. "What's happening, though?"

Donkey replied, "Man, a nigga done shot Dusty, and I need one of them K's."

Herman looked at him with a frown on his face and said, "A nigga done shot my Lil' cousin? Hold up a minute. I'll right back!" He opened the door of the house that he had stopped in front of and entered. He was in the house about five minutes and came out with an assault rifle under one arm, and another one hanging across his shoulders. He handed Donkey one of them.

A girl came up to the car and Donkey noticed that she was pregnant. She turned to Herman and asked him, "Herman, you ain't going to get in trouble, are you?"

He shouted, "No, Mary! Now go yo' ass inside!"

Mary stared at him for a minute and then asked, "What am I supposed to tell Alonzo if he calls?"

He looked at her and shouted back, "Just tell him I'll be back. Now, get yo' ass inside." She went inside and closed the door. Then Herman yelled out to a guy who was standing on the corner, "Say, Pie! Where y'all parked that car at?"

"'Round the corner in front of Angie's momma's Cadillac," replied Pie.

"Alright," Herman replied.

Herman and Donkey had driven off by the time Champ pulled up. He figured that at a time like this, if Donkey didn't turn to the gang, he would turn to his blood. He noticed Donkey's Eldorado parked in front of Herman's girlfriend's house. He pulled up to the corner, stopped and asked the guys, "Y'all know where the nigga went who was in this Eldorado?"

One of the guys replied, "Bruh, he and Herm shot outta here like bats outta hell!'

"Fuck!" Champ mumbled. He was upset because he had just missed them.

The guy added, "Something supposed to be going down because I saw them carry two of them noise makers with them."

"Yeah, I know. If they come back, tell them that Champ came by looking for them." The guy nodded.

The first place Donkey and Herm went was to Reggie's house in Uptown, known as the Tenth Ward. Donkey figured that Jay's friend from the football team was the one who shot Dusty. He wasn't playing any cat and mouse games. He figured Reggie would tell them what they needed to know. "Naw, Donkey Man," said Reggie as he sat in the back seat of the stolen car, "That nigga Jay was at practice until about five-thirty."

Donkey drove as he looked in the back mirror and asked, "Say bra, you sure that nigga was at-"

Herman interrupted Donkey, yelled, "Man, fuck that shit!", then turned around in his seat to look at Reggie. "Look here," he continued, "A nigga done shot my Lil' cousin on the real, and I'ma tell you straight up. I come to kill."

Reggie started to stutter, "Wha...wha? What he talking 'bout, Donk?"

Donkey replied, "Man, he's just tripping."

Reggie's eyes widened and he was scared as hell. "Man, look here," he yelled. "All I know is the shit that happened at school with your boy. But I don't know shit about the shooting!"

Donkey quickly looked back at Reggie and yelled, "Mutha fucka! You knew about that shit!" As he pulled the car to a stop on Washington Street near Magazine, he put the car in park and opened his door. Reggie started to look terrified as Donkey told him to get the fuck out, and Herman opened his door and got out as well. Reggie started walking around the car to Donkey while trying to explain himself. Donkey struck him in his face as soon as he was in striking distance and he fell to the ground. Reggie started trying to explain himself more, "It ain't what you think, man! It ain't what you think!"

Donkey walked back to the car to retrieve the screwdriver that they used to start the car. He placed it in the keyhole of the trunk. "What you doing, man?" a frightened Reggie asked Donkey, as the trunk of the car opened up. "If you just let me explain!" he continued.

Donkey said, "You done explained enough." Herm looked on while holding the assault rifle in his hand. Donkey reached inside of the trunk and pulled out a Louisville slugger.

Reggie saw the bat in Donkey's hands and yelled, "No, Donk! This Reggie, man!" he begged, as Donkey cocked the bat back and struck him on his knee. Reggie started screaming as he struck him again and again, repeatedly. With each blow, Reggie screamed out in pain. Donkey never said a word. Donkey just continued to hit him. He nearly beat him to death. Reggie's entire face was swollen beyond recognition and covered in blood. He could barely talk. Donkey had beaten him so much that Herman had to tell him to stop.

After beating Reggie, he tossed the bat into the trunk and walked around to the passenger's side of the car. He didn't feel much like driving anymore. Herm looked at Donkey as he sat in the car and asked, "What you trying to do, nigga?"

As he looked at Reggie, his hands were shaking like a leaf on a tree and Herm asked again, "Man, wha'cha want to do with this nigga?" Donkey never said a word and Herm hunched up his shoulders and said, "Fuck it then." Donkey then turned to Reggie, who was already in tremendous pain, and shot Reggie in his chest. Then he shot Reggie twice in the head.

A few hours after Reggie was killed, Donkey and Herm drove back to Herm's house in Nigger Town. The car that they were in was stolen, so Herman and his podnas kept it parked away from the house in case the police found it, so they wouldn't be able to link him to any crimes that had happened in it. Before Donkey left, Herm said, "Say bro, you gon' be alright, huh? I mean, it ain't shit for me to do around here. Fuck! I can sleep by you."

"Cuz," Donkey replied as he opened the door of his Eldorado, "Everything's cool, bro!" But we all knew it wasn't cool.

"Well the first thing that jumps off you, get to a phone and holler, okay? You know how I feel about my kinfolks," Herman replied.

Donkey started up the car and then looked at his cousin. With bloodshot eyes, Donkey said with a sneaky grin, "Yeah, nigga. I know."

"Holla at me when you get home, bra. So I will know that you made it."

"Nigger, your ass ain't gon' be woke!" answered Donkey.

"Shit!" replied Herman, "I'm going to jump up in me some ass," as he walked around the car and up on the front porch. Donkey closed the door while smiling, and drove off.

In other parts of the city, the gang had been searching for Donkey high and low. Busty had been riding around in an uptown neighborhood known as Zane City, hoping that he would come up with a little luck. As he drove up Erato Street he came onto Gayoso Street, where he saw this fella who went by the name Do Dirty, hanging out on the corner. He recognized him as being a regular buyer at the car wash. He was a rotten ex-con with a nasty drug habit, and was game to do whatever it took for the blast up the blood stream. Busty pulled his car to the curb, just about five feet from the corner, and reached over to grab his Colt 45 from the passenger seat. He would usually pack his pipe whenever he was in the presence of a fella such as Do Dirty. He just didn't give a fuck, and in his line of work, he didn't give many chances. He opened his car door, got out and walked over to Do Dirty. As he was walking over, he thought to himself, *Do Dirty has his people picked*.

"What's happening, young blood?" Do Dirty asked as he approached, "I wouldn't expect to see y'all up at this time of night."

Busty gave Dirty a firm handshake and said, "I'm out here looking for Donkey. You ain't seen him pass through here, did ya'?"

"You mean Pretty Boy? Yeah, he passed through here about an hour ago looking paranoid and shit."

"Was he alone?" asked Busty.

Do Dirty cocked his eye to the side and said, "Now, you know damn well Pretty Boy don't let no niggas ride in his shit, and all them Lil' ho's are inside. So what's that tell ya'?"

Busty glanced up the alley at an alley cat that he had spotted dashing across the street. Then he said, "Well look here, there was some player haters that passed by the car earlier today and put a hole in my Lil' brother's chest about the size of a softball."

"No! Not the Lil' one!" Do Dirty cried.

"Yeah, and he may not pull through," Busty replied as he went into his pocket and pulled out a twenty dollar bill. "So if you hear anything, just spin around by the car wash and holla at me. I'ma take care of ya." Busty handed him the bill, turned and got back in his car and pulled off.

After he had been gone for a while, Do Dirty walked around the corner and headed down Gayoso Street. He walked about half a block and then turned into an alley to a small apartment that sat behind the main house. He opened the screen door, knocked on the front door, and someone came to the door. The person peeped through a small windowpane beside it, noticed who it was, and opened the door.

A young female opened the door and as Do Dirty entered the house, she closed the door behind him and they walked into a room where three guys were sitting. One of them was the kid called Damian. He was lying back on a couch with a remote control in his hand. "What's up, nigga? I was about to call you anyway," Damian said as Do Dirty entered the room.

Do Dirty took off his coat and took a seat on the couch. One of the guys reached under the couch, and slid out a small mirror. On top of the mirror there was about half a package of heroin, a few syringes, a spoon, a small flamer, and some cotton balls. Damien tossed a thick rubber band to Do Dirty, who then sat the rubber beside him. He picked up one of the heroin packets. As Do Dirty opened it he said, "One of the Lil' niggers was out there." He then emptied the contents of the packets onto a spoon.

At this time a female stepped into the room, "Get the fuck out' here!" Damien screamed at her.

"I come to see if Brent was ready for his pain pills," the girl said. Damien looked over to the other side of the room at this kid who lay on his back on a small daybed with a neck brace on.

"He seems to be alright," Damien yelled. "Now get cho' ass outta here." She just stared at him. He then stood up from the couch and rushed toward her as she ran back into the other room. Once in the room, he began beating her. Her cries were heard in the main house, which was up front where his parents lived. They were both awakened from the cries coming from their son's apartment. His father said, "Sarah, he's beating her again!"

A tear ran down the side of his mother's face as she said, "Why doesn't she just leave?" as the cries continued. When he returned to the room, Do Dirty had three syringes filled with about twenty cc's of heroin apiece. Damien sat on the couch and said, "Pass me a rubber."

Do Dirty tossed the rubber band to him and he strapped it around his forearm. Then Damien said, "Come on! Fix me up."

Do Dirty gave him a strange look and said, "Young ass nigga. You don't know how to stick yourself?"

Damien just stared at him and said, "I just don't want to miss, bra!"

CHAPTER SEVEN

In another part of the city, Donkey was headed home after dropping his cousin Herman off in Pigeon Town. From where he was, he figured he would come out better slipping through Jefferson Parish and hopping on the Interstate to get to his house in Kenner. Kenner wasn't that far from the Old Carrollton area. Donkey had a lot of things on his mind. He was thinking about what his Lil' brother was going through. His cousin had just killed his best friend, and then he noticed the flashing of red lights in his rear-view mirror.

He pulled over to the curb and put his car in park, thinking that it was just his luck and that maybe they had just pulled him over on a routine traffic stop. As the policemen got out of their car and were walking over to his, Donkey pulled out his license and registration to have them ready. When the officers made it to his car, Donkey said, "I'm sorry, Officers. Was I speeding?"

As he handed his license to one of the officers, the other officer grabbed Donkey's belongings while looking into the car. He then looked over to his partner and said, "Hey, Tony. He asked me was he speeding!" And then they both start laughing.

Donkey then realized that something didn't look right and that's when the first officer said, "This is a nice Cadillac here. What line are you in?" as he looked at the gold medallion hanging from his neck and the nugget ring on his finger. Donkey saw what the officer was looking at and knew exactly where he was coming from so he said, "If you gon' write me out a ticket, then write it. If not, I really need to be going."

"Are you getting smart with me, boy? Cause I can take

your black ass in on no license and registration to this
vehicle," replied one of the officers.

Donkey looked back at the other officer who had his
license and registration in his hands and said, "Fuck you,
Rednecks!"

The officers stepped away from his car. They pulled out
their guns and said, "Sir! Will you please step out of your car
and put your hands where we can see them?"

"Fuck you! I'm a juvenile!" Donkey yelled as another
police car approached.

"Sir! Will you please hold your hands where I can see
them?" said the other cop.

"Fuck all you bitches! Shoot, mutha fucka! Shoot!" He
screamed as one of the officers walked up to his car and
opened his door. He resisted as they all pulled him out of
the car. They slammed him to the ground and cuffed him as
he continued to yell, "Fuck you, peckerwoods! Fuck you!"

Donkey was taken down to the Jefferson Parish Jail. His
day was already totally fucked up. Then on top of that, the
arresting officer booked him with no license, registration,
identification, no insurance, possession of a stolen vehicle,
resisting arrest by flight, and battery on a police officer. He
was booked under the name of John Doe. Donkey was only
fifteen at the time and wouldn't turn sixteen until the next
eight months. So he was placed in an adult facility because
the officer claimed that he was using an alias. He tried to tell
them who he was, but it seemed as if they were all in it
together. He was released into population and was scared as
hell, because all of the other convicts kept staring at him.
The deputy who took Donkey into population asked one of
the inmates, "Where's Dale?"

"I think he's in his cell sleeping, but if you want to know
where the empty cell at they got an opening for the fresh
meat in cell three and six," the inmate replied.

Donkey looked at the inmate as he spoke of fresh meat and then the deputy said to him "Well, you go ahead and camp out in cell six," and then he left.

As Donkey started toward the cell, he heard a guy in another cell say, "That boy got brown eyes just like my girl."

Then he heard another one say, "Welcome to hell, Lil' brother." Donkey was shaking like a leaf on a tree, because he knew that something was gonna jump off; he just didn't know when. As he entered the cell there was another inmate on his rack, sleeping. He didn't want to cause any problems by disturbing a man from his sleep so he lied down on his bed and just chilled. He lied in his bed for hours without a wink. He had heard some things about what happens in the pen and he was scared to sleep, but eventually he fell into a deep sleep.

Two days later, Dusty had pulled through his surgery like a true solider. Their mother, Ms. Gwen, was at his bedside when he first woke up. He looked at his mother and smiled. She asked, "Baby! How are you feeling?"

He sighed, "I've felt better."

Bruce said, "Damn, nigga! You had everybody thinking you were gon' die!"

Dusty smiled and said, "Hell. I thought I was gon' die, too."

Ms. Gwen stood up from her seat and picked up the phone while smiling and said, "Let me call your Pa, because he has been calling trying to find out how you were doing."

Dusty looked at Bruce and said, "That nigga Donkey, probably been driving y'all crazy, huh?" while grinning. Bruce just stared at him. His smile faded away, and Dusty knew that something had happened.

Dusty asked, "Say bro! Did something happen to Donk?" Bruce took a deep breath because he didn't want to lay it on him so soon, but he said, "Dusty, look. Everybody been trying to find him. We just don't know where he's at."

"You mean to tell me my brother is missing? Just like that, he can't be found?" replied Dusty. He was visibly worried. "He must be somewhere!"

Big Bruce replied, "He's been gone ever since you got shot."

"Gosh," Dusty sighed.

His mother said, "Baby, you want to talk to yo pa?"

Bruce stood up and headed for the door while saying, "Look, I'ma holla atcha later, bra."

"Yeah, cool," and then he left Dusty alone with his mom.

At the car wash, Busty and Bo were hanging around, watching the new crew work. Every now and then they'd help them out when they saw it was needed. Busty was telling Bo about this new female that he went out with last night and Bo said, "Say, bra. Man, I'm telling you! That's the same broad that used to live around by my Grandma's house."

"How the fuck you know the broad can't read, though?" shouted Busty.

"It was a long time ago. She probably can read a few words now," replied Bo, and they both started laughing.

"Nigga, fuck you," Busty mumbled as they watched Champ pull up in the parking lot.

"Alright!" yelled Bo, "We gon' ask Champ if he know her."

As Champ got out of his car and walked over to where they were, Bo said, "Now Champ, do you remember that broad around by Grandma's house that Bubble use to fuck with?"

Champ replied, "Who? Coniece?"

"Yeah, that's her!" Bo said.

"That girl can't even read," Champ added.

"I told you!" shouted Bo. "That's the same broad!"

"Alright, nigga! I believe," replied Busty, as Champ walked into the office.

Silk was sitting behind his desk when Champ walked in. "What's up, Silk?" he said, and headed to the back room. Champ returned with a soda in his hand and sat down on the edge of the desk. He took a sip out of it.

Silk looked up at him and said, "Champ! What the fuck is wrong with you?"

Champ turned and looked him and replied, "I'm just sitting on the desk."

Silk said, "Just look atcha, Champ! You haven't changed clothes in two days." Champ looked down at his clothes. "When the last time you been by Charlie's?" Silk asked.

"I don't need a haircut."

"Bullshit!" Silk shouted, "And you didn't sleep at home last night either!"

Champ was surprised, so he said, "Oh! You been watching me, huh?"

"No!" yelled Silk, "Sand gave me a call this morning. And I talked with Que, too. She said that she gave you four grand for three of them packages and you never showed up. You want to tell me about that?"

Champ got up from the desk, dropped the soda can in the trash, and told him, "She'll get it when I get over to it."

"Oh. That's how you take care of your business? When you want to, huh? They wait on you now, huh? You the man now, huh? That's how everything gon' go for now on? Champ's the man!" Silk yelled with sarcasm.

All of a sudden, Champ shoved the television off its stand and it smashed to the floor. Then he said, "Yeah, I'm the fucking man!" and rushed out of the office.

As Champ hurried passed Busty and Bo who were heading toward Silk's office, Silk yelled out at him, "Soldiers don't be slipping, Champ!" He got into his car and left.

Not long after Champ had left the car wash, Bruce arrived. He walked into the office and saw Bo sweeping the glass up from the busted television. He asked, "What the fuck happened here?"

Bo looked at him and replied, "That nigga Champ's trippin'."

Silk asked him, "How's everything at the hospital?"

"He came through today."

Silk looked at Bruce and asked, "You didn't mention Donkey to him, did ya?" Bruce just stood there in silence. "Damnit, Bruce!" cried Silk.

"I couldn't lie to him!" shouted Bruce, "He asked me, so I told him. But bra, ain't no butts about it. It would've gone the same way if the shoe was on the other foot." Silk was speechless because he knew that Bruce was right. But Silk had meant well. Bruce continued, "I've been thinking," as he sat down on the edge of the desk. "I don't think that I can handle this shit anymore, bra."

"What shit, Bruce?" Silk asked, as he looked on in suspense.

He turned to look at Silk and replied, "You know; this losing my people and shit." He pulled out his pistol from his waist and cocked it back. Silk and Bo just stared at him. "It was all cool in the beginning," he said, as he patted the pistol on his leg, "But it takes a player hater to come and fuck up shit." Tears began to roll down his face.

Silk could tell that there was a lot of anger and frustration built up inside of Bruce, but he was puzzled at his next question. "Why there have to be so many player haters, Silk?"

Silk stared at him, but didn't say a word. He figured he would let him get it all out and before long he continued, "Donkey is dead. Dusty is all fucked up. I mean, I'd give up all this shit if that's what it takes to keep my people safe!" He stood up from the desk and held his hands in the air. "A mutha fucka make you come out there, man! Can't y'all see this shit?"

Then he turned and aimed the pistol at the water cooler and starting shooting. Water went everywhere. He backed up against the wall and slid to the floor. Busty ran into the office and looked down at Bruce, and knew exactly what was on his mind. After he had released all of his steam, Silk had a long talk with him about the game. He explained to him that that was part of the game. Everything was included, and nobody understood that.

Back in Jefferson Parish Jail, Donkey had survived through the first couple of days. Since he was booked as a John Doe, he wasn't entitled a phone call. This was an obvious violation of his constitutional rights. And in turn, he couldn't post bail because he couldn't get in touch with anyone. There were two guys in a cell talking, "Say Dale," one of the guys said while playing a game of solitaire on his bunk, "Pass me one of those Cadillacs, nigga."

"Hold up. It's under the foot of my rack," replied the other guy, who was sitting toward the end of the bunk. He stood up and lifted the foot of the mattress on the top bunk. He pulled out a pack of Kool filtered King's cigarettes. He lit it, puffed on it and exhaled a thick cloud of smoke. Then he handed it to Dale, who grabbed it and placed it in his mouth, then continued the game.

The first guy said, "Dale, how come you ain't been hollering at yo boy, Jones?"

"Man! Mutha fuck Jones!" Dale replied as he reached under his pillow to retrieve an envelope. "All those free folks are the same," he added as he opened up the envelope and pulled a letter out. "Want to have this Podman, the police shit, ya' know?" As he unfolded the letter he continued, "Pony, I ain't come here to be no Rat, 'cha know?"

Pony replied, "I'm hip, Dale. I'm hip!" Dale read the letter.

"Another one of those headaches, huh?" Dale said as he read, "She just telling me about my Lil' cousin Nawdy."

"Oh, the Lil' nigga in the paper?" asked Pony.

"Yeah, she said some mutha fucka identified him as the trigger man." Dale folded the letter up, placed it back in the envelope and slid it back under his pillow. "Young ass niggas don't be thinking," he added.

"Dale, man. You know how them juveniles do. It ain't like when we was young," said Pony.

"I'm hip," replied Dale, as he rested back on his bunk.

Pony put the cigarette out in a homemade ash tray made out of aluminum foil. Then then said, "I been checking that Lil' youngster out who came in the other day. Have you seen him?"

"Yeah, I saw him," replied Dale.

"The Lil' nigga look like he'd fight for that ass, if a nigga tried to take it," said Pony.

"Yeah. He'd fight for it," replied Dale. "They all gon' put up a fight." As he got up and walked to the cell door, he looked down toward Donkey's cell. "But is he willing to die for it?" he added.

Back in New Orleans, Kay and Damien were arguing outside of Jane Lee's salon, "How come I haven't seen you in three days?"

Damien replied, "I've been calling yo' house every day!"

"So why you ain't pass over here? You know what I wanted to talk to you about," Kay said.

"What you want to talk to me about? That Lil' shit at the car wash again? I told you don't worry about that shit," said Damien.

"You told me to handle it. So I handled it!" Kay stood with her arms folded.

"I told you to fuck with Champ, not Dusty!" he yelled.

"Then you ain't have to shoot him!" said Kay.

Then what you wanted me to do?" shouted Damien, as he opened up his arms wide. "Oh, I see now. You got feelings for this nigga. So when you and him fall out you call on me to come and rough him up a Lil' bit, huh?"

"I ain't say that!" replied Kay. "I just didn't expect you to kill him like that."

Damien stepped closer to Kay, grabbed her around her waist and said, "Look here, next time I'ma just-"

Kay cut him off, "Ain't gon' be a next time!"

"Alright, alright," said Damien. "I ain't gon' fuck with the Lil' nigga no more. But in the meantime, I want you to keep all this hush-hush, ya hear me? Cause I don't want to have to do it to you!" Then he walked to his car, got in and pulled away. Tears started running down her face as she stood watching him ride down the block. Even after he was out of sight, she still stood there crying.

In the Irish Channel, a neighborhood near the river also known as the Eleventh Ward, Busty was riding around trying to find the address of the girl's house whom he had recently met. He was coming down Phillip Street near Annunciation Street when he decided to pull to the side and get some directions from these guys who were hanging out in front of one of the houses on the corner. He pulled to the curb, rolled down his window and said, "Bra, y'all know a broad name Coniece that just moved around here?" They all nodded their heads yes.

One guy asked, "What hundred block do she live in?"

Busty pulled out a piece of paper from the ashtray and said, "She stay at four-thirty-two Phillip."

The guy looked down the street and said, "Well, that's the four-hundred block down there, bro. So, what you can do is check the places for her address."

"Alright. I appreciate it, bro," Busty said as he pulled off.

When Busty got to the block, he parked his car, got out and looked for the house on foot. He knew that the even numbers were on one side and the odds were on the other. He walked on the even side. 428, 430... he kept looking and then he stopped. "Man, what the fuck is going on round here?" he mumbled to himself as he looked up at the addresses. Four-thirty-two was missing. The numbers had jumped from 430 to 434. He was puzzled. Then the guy who gave him the directions on the other corner rode up the street on a ten-speed bicycle. Busty turned to look at him and said, "Say, bro, they don't even have any four-thirty-two."

The guy looked up at the address and saw that 432 wasn't there. He said, "Oh, four-thirty-two must be in the back."

Busty walked over to look through the alley. In the back, he saw a mailbox and some potted plants beside the door. He went through the alley and saw 432. He then turned and gave the guy a signal that he had found the house, and the guy rode away. Busty knocked on the door and somebody asked, "Who is it?"

"Do Coniece live here?" Busty asked. Somebody unlocked the door and opened it. It was Coniece. She stood there with a long Mickey Mouse shirt and a pair of cut jean shorts, smiling at him. They were cut off so short that it sort of reminded him of the girl on *Dukes of Hazard*, Daisy.

She said, "Yo' ass probably been trying to find this house for hours, huh?" with a sassy grin.

"Yeah! I've been riding around here for a Lil' while," he said.

"You should have told me you were coming. I would've been standing out there waiting for you," said Coniece.

Busty asked, "Why you ain't staying by yo' momma house?"

She just looked at him at first and then said, "She be trying to be too strict and shit. I'm grown up now and I can't be having that. Why, that's what you come over here to ask me?"

Busty smiled, "Naw! I just come to spend a little time wit' cha. You ain't gon' invite me in?" he asked.

Suddenly, the happy-to-see-you look turned into a look of embarrassment. She turned to look back at the house, then back at Busty. Quickly, he realized that she was ashamed of something, and then she said, "Busty, look-"

"No! You look, Coniece! You don't have to be embarrassed about anything around me because I have been there before. I ain't worried about how you living. I come here to see you. Now you gon' let me in, or what?"

Coniece just stared at Busty, as if searching for something, and then she slowly said, "Come on in."

She opened the door wide so that he could come in. When he walked into the house, he saw exactly what she was ashamed of. He looked around the room. He saw a pillow on a ragged plaid couch in the middle of the room and he figured that this is where she slept. There was a small 10-inch black and white television sitting on top of a milk crate on the opposite side of the couch. Horizontal lines ran up the screen. The floor of the room was covered with an old, shaggy, olive-green carpet that was filthy. In the far corner, there was a rather large rattrap and it was set up for the catch. As she closed the door, Busty turned to look at her and she finally said in a low tone, "You feel me."

"Yeah," he replied. "I feel ya." Then a door that led to another part of the house opened. "Coniece, was somebody knocking?" asked another female as she came through the door, spotting Busty.

She was half-naked. The only thing she had on was a pair of satin red panties. She looked as good as Coniece, with an even better figure. She looked Busty up and down, and she liked what she saw. He looked at her firm breasts, thin waistline, nice hips, and the puff-out imprint of her bush in the front of her panties, but he wasn't amused. He frowned up and said, "I ain't come here to see yo' naked ass." Her slight flirty expression turned pale. Busty continued, "So if you don't mind."

Coniece looked on as the girl turned and went back into the room. She started laughing as she walked over to the couch and sat down. Busty sat down next to her and said, "Ain't that a bitch," as he looked over at her.

"This is her house," said Coniece.

"I don't give a fuck!" Busty said, "Respect is due all over the world. So her house doesn't change anything."

Back in Zane City by Damien's house, his mother had walked to the back to ask her sons' girlfriend, Peaches (who was home alone), if she wanted to join them for dinner up front in the big house. Peaches agreed and went up to the main house. While they were having dinner, Damien's mother said, "Now, baby, Damien is my son and this is true, but you can't let him control your life."

His father stuffed a spoon of corn bread dressing into his mouth while looking at Peaches. After digesting it, he said, "You know sweetheart, what you need to do is call them damn white folks on his ass!"

"Naw, Harold!" his mother said abruptly, "How can you sit there and say that? All she needs to do is leave his ass back there!" She said as she sipped on a glass of sweet tea.

In a motel in an uptown area called Madison, Damien and Kay were checking into a room, "How much for the room?" he asked.

The desk clerk replied, "How long do you plan on staying?" Damien looked at Kay, then at his watch and then replied, "About three hours."

"Then that'll be twelve dollars. You get five dollars back if you return the key within six hours."

Damien mumbled, "We'll be out way before then," as he reached into his pocket and pulled out a ten-dollar bill. He put the bill on the counter then searched in his pocket for two dollars, and after realizing he didn't have any more money, he turned to look at Kay. She just stared at him.

"You don't have two dollars?" he asked and she rolled her eyes at him. Then she went into her purse, pulled out a five-dollar bill, and sat it on the counter. The desk clerk grabbed the money, went into his register, and gave Kay three dollars back. As she grabbed the money, the desk clerk looked at her and shook his head from side to side.

"Darling, maybe you ought to go back home," said Damien's mother, "Because I can't stand hearing him beat on you like that. Don't you have a family that you can go home to?"

She gathered up all the empty dinner plates and headed for the sink. Peaches never responded. She just sipped on the sweet tea and stared at a hickory chopping board that hung from a nail on the wall in the kitchen that read "Mom's Kitchen."

At the motel, Kay was sitting on the edge of the bed getting undressed. She unbuttoned her blouse from the back and slipped it off. Her firm breasts were erect as the imprints of her nipples poked out through her bra. The lace bikini that she wore had run up the crack of her ass. She pulled the covers of the bed back and got under them. She fluffed up the pillows for comfort and then she laid back on them.

"Let me tell you something, Sweetheart," Damien's father

said to Peaches. "I been married to my wife for twenty-seven years."

"And he never touched me once," Damien's mother said.

"Goddammit, Ruby!" yelled the father.

"Go ahead, Harold!" Ruby yelled. "Say wha'cha got to say. Shit!"

She began to wipe the table with a towel. Harold said, "For twenty-seven years I been with my wife and never hit her. My oldest son Harold Jr., God bless his soul, he killed many people and I knew it, but I still took his side no matter what. But it's three types of mutha fuckas I hate," he added as he looked at Peaches. "A thief, a rapist, and a damn woman-beater!"

Kay was waiting for Damien to come out of the motel bathroom. Inside the bathroom, Damien was sitting on the toilet with a syringe with five cc's of heroin in it, stuck in his arm. He pushed the heroin into his veins slowly. He raised his head to look at the ceiling as he savored the feeling that the heroin gave him; he loved it so much. Sweat ran down his face like raindrops, as he pulled the syringe from his arm and rested back on the toilet to enjoy the effect of the potency. He then stood up, pulled a handkerchief from his back pocket and wiped the sweat from his face. He turned the knob on the door and walked out of the bathroom.

"Baby, tell me something," said Mrs. Ruby as she looked to the front of the house for her husband, who moments before had stepped out of the kitchen. "Is the sex really that good?" Peaches had a look on her face that sort of answered her question without speaking. "Lord, have mercy on this child!" Mrs. Ruby sighed. "The next thing you gon' tell me is you in love, huh?" Peaches held her head down. "I know just how you feel, baby. You laid down once and couldn't get up. Well, take some advice from a woman who has been there."

Peaches raised her head to look at her for the first time. "Baby, time's been valuable since the days of Christ, and it's worth way more than a few dollars and a good feeling. All that just makes things a little better but what a woman really need is quality time and loving care. Which means as nice-looking as you is, you must be playing with half a deck," Peaches looked at her, curious. Mrs. Ruby continued, "My son don't provide you with any quality time because he stay running the streets. You ain't getting any loving care because he beats on you. The few dollars you see every now and then, well I hope you don't consider that money," and then she looked into Peaches eyes and said, "So baby, you ain't getting nothing but a Lil' sex out of the deal."

"Oh! Oh! Damien!" screamed Kay, as he lay on top of her, stabbing his cock into her ruthlessly. Her legs were stretched out as wide as they could go and her fingernails clawed into his back. Her mouth was wide open, as well as her eyes, as she screamed in enormous pain. He had one hand on the top of the headboard and the other on the edge of the bed for balance as he thrust inside of her. "Oh! Damien, stop! Please, Damien! It's burning! It's burning!" she started yelling.

Blood began to run from her vagina and onto the bed. Tears ran down her face as she continued to scream for him to stop, but he didn't stop. He started pushing inside her even harder, while making facial expressions, his abilities being pushed to the limits. Blood continued to run from her vagina and the smell of fresh blood filled the room. After realizing that he wasn't going to stop until he reached satisfaction, Kay just relaxed and let him do his thing.

In the Irish Channel at Coniece's house, Busty was about to leave. He walked to the door when she asked, "You about to go?"

He looked at her and replied, "Yeah. I'm about to slide. I'ma holla at cha."

Coniece sat with a disappointed look on her face. Busty noticed it and said, "You don't know what to think, huh."

She looked away because she couldn't give him eye contact out of shame. He walked back over to the couch, sat beside her, and lifted her chin up so he could look her in her eyes. She began to fiddle with some loose strings on her cut-off shorts.

"When I told you that I felt you, I meant that. I get that you been doing it for so long to survive that it's become your habit," he said. He grabbed her hand and placed it on his and said, "I know that I can get that there whenever I want," as he pointed to her crotch. "But, uh, let's let everything fall into place." He placed his hand on the back of her neck and pulled her to him to press his lips against hers. They shared a long, passionate kiss. "I'ma holla at you tomorrow, okay?" Busty asked.

She answered, "Okay," in a low tone.

He left and she lay back on the couch, smiling. She felt wanted. She felt special, like she had never felt in her life. She had always looked at herself as a whore.

Peaches had finished talking with Damien's mother and started for the door. Before she opened the door, she turned to Mrs. Ruby and said, "Thank you for dinner. I really had a nice time talking to you," she added.

"Well, I know you gon' do the right thing, but I want you to know, I'ma stand behind you in what decision you make," Mrs. Ruby said.

"Damien should be home soon, so I must be going now," Peaches replied. She turned and walked out the door. Mrs. Ruby started mumbling The Lord's Prayer as she watched her walk through the alley toward the back apartment.

Damien was on his way to bring Kay home after leaving the motel. He was headed down Washington Avenue nearing Magnolia, when he stopped at a traffic light. Kay hadn't said a word since they left the motel. He looked over at her, as she kept looking out of the window. "So you don't want to talk to me?" he asked, and she didn't respond. "Come on Kay, say something to me," and he placed his hand on her shoulder to rub her hair.

She quickly brushed his hands away from her and continued to stare out the window. The traffic light turned green and he attempted to cheer her up. "Don't touch me!" she shouted, as a motorist starting honking his horn from behind. He smashed on the gas and continued up Washington Street. At Willow Street, he made a quick left turn into the Magnolia Projects. Then at about half of a block down, he pulled to the side near the courtyard. He put the car in park and struck Kay in her face, giving her a backhand punch sending her head into the passenger side window. She made a loud scream as Damien snatched her by her hair and started punching her in her face repeatedly. She screamed and screamed as he continued to punch her in her face and pull her hair. Next, he jerked her head toward him and then shoved it back into the passenger side window, shattering the glass.

He reached over, opened the passenger door, and shoved her out of the car. She fell into the street with her face covered with blood. "I been too good to you, bitch!" he shouted as he slammed the door and pulled off.

"And when I get that feeling, I want Sex-u-al healing…" Marvin Gaye sang on the car radio.

"So you and Bianca was up at the hospital all day?" asked Champ as he and Sand cruised in his Eldorado, listening to the smooth music.

"Yeah. We up there until about nine-thirty," Sand replied.

"Was he talking to y'all?" asked Champ.

"Uh-huh. He kept talking 'bout Kiwanna," Sand replied. "He really likes that Lil' girl, huh?"

"Yeah, that's his Lil' squeeze," he replied as he glanced over at her. She had kicked off her shoes and her legs were folded up in the seat. Her short jean mini skirt raised above her thigh showing the imprint of her vagina, as it puffed out of her satin panties. Champ was driving down South Claiborne Avenue and made a left turn at Jackson, heading toward Galvez. When he made it to South Johnson, he saw Damien's car parked on the corner so he looked around as he drove by. He didn't see him. He didn't have anything against Damien, but he wanted to talk to him to see if he had heard anything about Donkey's whereabouts. After all, Donkey would always be hanging out with him and that kid Reggie who was recently killed. He figured if the three of them had a problem with someone that resulted in Reggie and Donkey getting killed, he thought that he was entitled to know about it.

Champ drove a block and pulled in front of Damien's old eighty-one Camaro, then cut off his lights. He reached under his seat to retrieve his gun as he turned to look at Sand, because he had promised her that he would not use a gun. They stared into each other's eyes for a minute because she was dwelling on the promise, and he was dwelling on a habit. "Where ever I go," he said in a low tone, "I take it with me."

She just smacked her lips, rolled her eyes, and turned the other way. Champ got out of the car and closed the door behind him. He stuffed the .45 Magnum in his pants, walked to the Camaro and looked inside the windows. On the other side, he saw the passenger side window had been shattered and he mumbled, "First Reggie and Donkey, now you?"

While walking around to the other side of the car, he noticed that there was blood on the passenger side window. *Who the fuck's doing this shit?* He asked himself as a noise came from a nearby alley. He looked over toward the alley and then at his car. He noticed that Sand heard the noise, too. It sounded like fumbling aluminum cans of some sort. His car was directly in front of the alley, but it was too dark to see anything. Sand couldn't see but a foot or two in the alley. Champ pulled his pistol out, cocked the hammer back, and then started walking toward the alley. As soon as he made it, something rushed out of it. He stepped back and got ready for the kill, when he noticed that it was just a stray alley cat. It scared the hell out of him and Sand. He un-cocked his gun and walked to his car, and they left. "I'll catch up to Damien another time," he thought.

CHAPTER EIGHT

In the Jefferson Parish Jail, Donkey had decided to take a shower before he crashed out. He got his things together and had a nice, warm shower. He expected a problem, but there wasn't any at all. After taking a shower, he wrapped his drying towel around his waist, grabbed his soap, and headed back to his cell. As he passed by the Pod man's cell, Dale and Pony were standing by the bars of their cell watching him. By Donkey being young and in an adult facility, he was paranoid about a lot of things, and that was one of them. He thought that they were looking at his ass.

"The Lil' nigga gotta complex," Dale said to Pony in a low tone.

"Uh huh," replied Dale, "He young, you know."

Donkey was in cell three and Dale and Pony were watching him from cell nine, but there was someone else watching him, too. In cell eleven there were two more guys standing at their cell bars watching him. "You think this Lil' nigga scared to bleed, Dog?" one of the men asked.

"He don't have to," said the other guy. "I done stuck a solider before Hank. You know my background," as he walked over to his bunk and reached under his pillow and pulled out a homemade blade.

In the system, his weapon is called a shank or a tool. He rotated it in the palm of his hand making the reflection from the cell light in his face. It was a sharp piece of a metal object about five inches long, with tape around one end that was used to grip the handle. He walked back to the bars and mumbled, "Its gon' be a long night, youngsta, a long night!"

Once in his cell, Donkey starting putting on his clothes when the guy in the cell asked, "Lil' man, where did you say you were from?" as he lay back on his bunk.

"I'm from Uptown," he said, as he hung his face towel on the edge of his bunk.

"Oh! You should know Halloween, then! Cause he's from Uptown," his celly said.

"Naw, bro. I don't know any nigga by the name of Halloween," replied Donkey.

Then the guy said, "If you were hustling man, then you should know him. Cause he be playing with a lot of coke, you know."

Donkey turned to look at his celly. It was then that he realized how far and how fast a player's business could travel. "Man, I work at a car wash," Donkey said, as he started laughing. He then thought that he would brush his teeth before he crashed, so he lifted the end of his mattress to get his toothbrush and toothpaste, but instead he saw something else. It was a shank and he looked around to see if anyone was watching him. He wondered where it had come from. This shank was different from the one the guy had in cell eleven. It was double in length and width, and as he grabbed it he started smiling. He had once stabbed a man to death, so doing it again to protect his manhood didn't mean shit to him. He grabbed the shank from his bed and showed it to his celly. "Is this yours?" he asked.

His cellmate's eyes widened to the sight of it, and he replied, "Naw, Lil' man, it ain't mine. Why?"

Donkey placed the shank back under the mattress and said, "I looked under my mattress and it was just there."

"Say Lil' man," the guy said as Donkey turned to look at him. "Prepare yourself! You've been marked!"

Kay was rushed to Charity Hospital of New Orleans. Someone was walking down Willow Street through the Magnolia Projects, saw her, and called for an ambulance. "Coming through! Coming through!" a doctor yelled, as they rushed her to the ICU Unit yelling, "I need anesthesia! I need two hundred and fifty cc's of Morphine and oxygen!"

Another yelled as he placed an oxygen mask over Kay's face, "Have Doctor Payne meet me in surgery!" he yelled to another, "Quickly! Quickly!"

Later that night in the Jefferson Parish Jail, "Go ahead, Hank! Handle yo' business," said Dog, as he stood in the door of his cell with his shank cuffed behind his leg.

Hank walked out of his cell and went up to the guard's booth where Pony was talking to a deputy. "Say Pony," and he turned around to look at him, "Would you lend me two packs of cigarettes for four store days?" asked Hank.

Pony and Dale were always open for a hustle. Pony replied, "Alright! I'll drop 'em in your cell."

"Dog gon' get' em," said Hank as he started toward his cell.

Once he was in his cell, Hank turned to look at the Deputy and said, "Close everything except six and eleven," and it was done. As the cells began to close, Pony and Dale ran up to the bars because they knew that something was about to go down. Donkey was lying under his cover with the shank in his hand when Dog walked out of his cell, with a shank in his right hand. He grabbed the blanket with his left hand and snatched it from over Donkey's head. Without any warning, like a snake, Donkey rose up with the shank and stuck Dog in his neck. Dog jumped back and put his hand on his neck, as his blood poured through his fingers. The sharp blade had cut his jugular vein like a cantaloupe. Donkey leaped out of his bunk and charged him again. Dog came swinging his shank with his right hand, putting a cut across Donkey's face about nine inches long. It came from below his left ear lobe and ended over his right eye.

Donkey jumped to the side and held his hand over his face. Somebody yelled, "Blood!"

Then all the inmates started shouting, "Blood! Blood!"

Dog began to laugh at Donkey, saying, "I want it, Lil' nigga!"

Donkey charged him again. Dog came across with the shank again. He cut Donkey, leaving a gash about half the size of the first one. It started at his right cheekbone, went under his right eye and across his nose about an inch. This time, Donkey didn't stop. He stuck the blade into Dog's left rib cage on an upward angle. Dog screamed out in pain, dropped the shank, and placed his hands around Donkey's neck. Donkey pulled the shank back and stabbed him again and again and again, until a gang of deputies ran into the cell to restrain him.

The cell floor was filled with blood and his face and clothes were covered with blood as the deputies dragged Donkey out of the cell. Pony and Dale looked on. Since he was still alive, they knew that he had come out on top of the situation. Pony said, "Dale, it's a good thing you slipped that blade under that Lil' nigga bunk. He caught a few bad ones up in there."

"Uh huh!" replied Dale, "But Dog will never get well."

At four o'clock the following morning, Champ and Sand had just hopped out of the shower, after finishing three and a half hours of hot sex. He lay down in the bed as he watched her stand in the mirror and blow her hair dry. She wore burgundy Victoria Secret undergarments. As the small bikini panties slid up her ass crack, she turned to look at him. He had his hand sitting over his john, and she said, "We ain't doing it no more. Nasty!" and he started laughing.

The phone rang and Sand said, "Now, it's four o'clock in the morning."

Champ reached over the bed to get the phone. He said. "Hello?"

"Donkey's on the news!" It was his mother. She had been

up doing what she usually did at four o'clock in the morning: looking at the news, and drinking her coffee. When she saw Donkey on the news, she called Champ. He grabbed the remote control from the middle of the bed and turned on the television.

"This is John Snell, and this is your morning news," said the news anchor. "Jefferson Parish authorities have been trying to come up with some answers to piece together their latest homicide," as he flipped through some papers that sat in front of him. "Well, sources say a man arrested in Jefferson Parish some days ago on a string of traffic violations was taken to the Jefferson Parish Jail and released into population. While in population, the man was involved in a knife fight, which resulted in the death of another man. This man was placed in isolation and rebooked for first-degree murder and it was then that authorities realized that the man is actually a juvenile."

Donkey's picture showed up on the screen and Sand yelled out, "That's Donkey!"

The anchorman continued, "This is the juvenile. His name is unknown at this time so if anyone recognizes this man, please contact the Jefferson Parish Sheriff's Office at the number on your screen."

At 8:00 AM, four hours later, Minnie and Jane Lee stood over Kay's hospital bed, weeping. She lay unconscious with bandages around her head. The sound of an oxygen respirator pumping up and down filled the room. Jane Lee placed her hand on her head gently while mumbling, "Be strong for Momma," as she looked at her daughter's badly damaged face.

Her eyes were swollen and her cheeks were this purplish color and even more swollen, which made her face look fat. Her godmother Glo walked into the hospital room along with her husband, June, at about 8:22 AM. She said, "Jane

Lee, where is my baby?" When she saw how badly Kay had been beaten, she yelled with despair, "Oh no, Lord!"

Glo turned to grab hold of her husband. "Lord, have mercy on my godchild!" she screamed.

June braced his arms around her and said, "Be strong, Glo. Be strong." His eyes were tearing up, too.

"My baby!" Glo cried out.

"Lord, that's my baby!" Jane Lee dropped to her knees beside the bed with a loud cry, and placed her hands over her face. She started rocking back and forth. Minnie broke out in a loud cry. It was a terrible moment of sorrow.

"They wouldn't let anybody in the room to talk to him except his momma," Silk said to Redd when he arrived at Meta Crest Hospital in Jefferson Parish, where Donkey was taken for treatment for the slash across his face.

"All those damn reporters in there!" shouted Redd. "And his own damn family can't see him!" he said as he began to get frustrated.

"They talking about this immediate family shit," replied Silk, as Champ and Bruce walked up. The whole group had been there since about four thirty or five o'clock AM. Silk asked, "What they screaming, Champ?" as he turned around and look toward the room.

"All I could get was a peek at him. Damn deputies don't want anybody near the room. His face is all wrapped up and shit," Champ replied.

Then Donkey's mother exited the room and walked over to where everyone was waiting. Silk asked as she approached, "What did they say, Maggie?"

She looked into his eyes and said, "Get an Attorney."

CHAPTER NINE

In the office of attorney Roger Dawson, the sign on the door read Dawson and Marcello's Law Firm. "What we have here is a class-action lawsuit against the Jefferson Parish Sheriff's Office," said Mr. Dawson as he sat behind his desk.

"Will you take the case?" asked Silk, as he stood along with Mrs. Maggie, Redd, and Redd's partner Leroy White, who had introduced them to Mr. Dawson.

"Well," replied Mr. Dawson, "I am qualified to handle this case but I must tell you that it will take time and money."

"How much?" asked Silk and Redd, almost simultaneously.

Mr. Dawson he looked them in the eyes and replied, "About fifteen grand to begin with."

At the home of Wallace King, the Mayor of Jefferson Parish, an intense conversation was going down. "Godamnit, Burt!" the Mayor shouted as he paced his in home office back and forth, "How could you make such a simple mistake?"

Burt replied, "I didn't know about it."

Mayor King was livid. "How can you not know about it?" he shouted abruptly. "You're the damn Sheriff, for cryin' out loud!" He stopped to look Burt in his eyes and asked, "Do you know what this is going to cost this parish? Not to consider your job, or my position?" Burt just held his head down in regret.

Roger Dawson picked up the phone and called an associate of his at the Internal Affairs Office. "Yes. Kyle Dawson here. I have something that I would like to discuss with you," said Dawson as he looked at the fifteen thousand dollars in cash lying in front of him on his desk. "Okay. Will meet you at Café Du Monde at three o'clock," he said as he hung up the phone. He looked up at Silk and said, "We're on!"

Over at the mayor's house, Burt listened as Mayor King spoke. "Burt, I want you to find out everything you can about that kid. Do you hear me?"

Burt nodded. "Yes, Sir," he replied.

The mayor wanted to make sure Burt got the message loud and clear. "I mean everything!" he added, shouting. "Find out what pussy he dropped from, to how many cavities he has in his mouth!"

Burt replied, "But Mr. Mayor, the kid's residence is in Orleans Parish."

The mayor looked at Burt and asked, "Is that a problem, Burt? Is it?"

"No, Sir!" said Burt. "It's no problem!"

Over at the house of Judge Morgan J. Reedley, Mr. Dawson conferred with the judge. "So what you are asking me is to have a man released who's been booked for murder? On my behalf?" asked Judge Reedley.

Mr. Dawson nodded his head and replied, "Yes, your honor."

"Under what grounds?" asked Judge Reedly. Mr. Dawson then walked over to his briefcase which sat on a nearby table and laid it down. He opened the briefcase and pulled out some papers and pictures of Donkey, which were taken after the incident.

Mr. Dawson said, "Your Honor, my client was placed in an adult facility as a minor." He then placed the papers and photographs on the desk in front of the judge.

The judge picked up the photos of Donkey and said, "My God! What happen to him?"

"Your honor, my client's life was jeopardized by another inmate, which resulted in him killing another man," replied Mr. Dawson.

Judge Reedley asked, "And you say that your client is a juvenile?"

"Yes, your Honor," replied Mr. Dawson.

"Very well then, Mr. Dawson. I will authorize his release. I would not want him to go through any more than he has already endured," the judge stated. He set the photographs back on the desk.

Mr. Dawson had a talk with a judge and had him get Donkey released from jail on his behalf, but he had to wait a couple of days before he was discharged from the hospital.

Kay had pulled through from the beating and on the morning that she woke up, Jane Lee and her best friend from school were at her side. Her mom had to feed her because after three days of unconsciousness, Kay was still very weak.

"I can't believe that Lil' mutha fucka," Jane Lee said as she stuffed a spoonful of wheat cereal into Kay's mouth. "You should've stayed with that other Lil' boy, Kay. What's his name?" she continued.

Kay's friend Brenda replied, "His name is Champ!"

Then Brenda started daydreaming; she thought about the time Kay used Damien to try and make Champ jealous at the car wash. Damien had just come from picking up Kay and Brenda from Jane Lee's salon, and Reggie was with him.

As they passed by the car wash, Kay said, "Go up in there!"

Damien had looked over at Kay, who was seated in the front and said, "You just want to fuck with that Lil' nigga, huh?" Kay started laughing and Damien smiled at her as he pulled into the car wash. Champ walked over to the car as it stopped. Damien had then rolled down the window and said, "Just wipe it, dog-"

"Brenda!" shouted Jane Lee, interrupting Brenda's daydream. "Girl! You ain't hear me talking to you?" Jane Lee asked.

"No," replied Brenda.

Jane Lee continued, "I'm about to run downstairs and get something to eat. Do you want something?" she asked Brenda.

"No, I'm al 'right she," replied; Jane Lee left.

When Donkey got home, he wanted to see his 'Lil brother first. As soon as he walked into the room, Dusty began with, "What's up, nigga?" Dusty explained that the rest of the gang wasn't there because he had wanted to talk to Donkey alone.

"Lil' brother, you know me," replied Donkey as he walked over and hugged him tight. "I'm a solider in the flesh, bro," he said as he opened his arms out wide.

Dusty asked, "What happen to your face, bro?"

"Man, fuck that," replied Donkey, "What's up with you?"

Dusty looked at his brother for a moment and then he started smiling, saying, "Ah, nigga. They about to cut me loose in six days." Then he started moving around a bit to show Donkey that he was feeling alright. "Doc says I'ma catch a few headaches here and there, but I'm cool," he said as Donkey grabbed a chair and pulled it closer to the bed.

Donkey said, "Yo Lil' bitch ain't come holla at cha?" as he sat in the chair and cocked his legs up on the edge of the bed.

"Hey, boy," said Dusty, "You better watch how you speak about my queen!" And they both started laughing.

"Alright, your majesty," Donkey added, and Dusty laughed again.

But then, Dusty noticed Donkey was staring straight at him, and his laugh had quickly faded away. "What? What you looking at me like that for?" asked Dusty.

Donkey just stared out the window and then back at his brother then said, "Bro, I almost lost you." Then there was a moment of silence.

"Yeah bro, I understand. But I don't think I'ma go like that," Dusty replied. "Nigga! When I go, I'ma be smoking on a bomb reefer and I'ma be laid back in a piece of ass."

Donkey looked at him and said, "Naw, nigga! You ain't going out like that."

After a moment, Dusty asked, "Then how I'ma go?"

He was looking curiously over at his brother and Donkey replied, "Nigga, you gon' be riding with me." Dusty smiled.

"Alright, that cool," he said. "But I still want to be high." They chuckled.

After visiting Dusty, Donkey went home. Bianca was very was glad to see him. He took a nice, hot shower and walked into the bedroom. He clicked on the television and lay back in his bed. Bianca, who was sitting on the other side of the bed, was full of curiosity because she wanted to know about the bizarre experience he had been through in the days past. Donkey never mentioned it however, or in any way showed her that he had missed making love to her, or that he had missed her at all. "Let me see," she said as she looked over at him.

He glanced over at her and then back at the television. Then he asked, "Let you see what?"

She replied in a soft tone, "I want to see your face, bae." He was silent for a moment and then turned to look directly into her eyes. She really wanted to see what his face looked like under the bandages. He sat the remote control down beside the bed, and raised his hands up to his face. Slowly, Donkey started peeling off the mask-like bandages and Bianca looked on in suspense. When he had peeled all of the bandages off, he turned to look Bianca directly in her eyes. The long cut over his right eye and across his face to his left ear, and the shorter one that came from over his nose to his right cheekbone all combined formed an upside down Y-shaped scar.

Donkey said, "Look, let me put the-" and she grabbed his hand quickly as he attempted to put the bandage back on.

"It don't matter to me," she said as she came closer to him. "I love you," Bianca continued, and then she kissed him.

After sharing a long overdue, passionate kiss, Donkey mumbled, "Chill."

This took Bianca by surprise. She leaned back to look at him. "What's wrong?" she asked as he got up off the bed and walked over to the dresser to look in the mirror. He placed his hand in his face and ran it over the scars gently. He stood, staring at himself in the mirror, mesmerized. Then his mind started drifting. He was having a flashback of the past. Donkey suddenly felt as if he was back in his childhood, standing in his local childhood grocery store.

FLASHBACKS:

"Hey, Donkey!" said Mr. Lee, "Where is your Lil' brother?"

Donkey told Mr. Lee that his brother was back at home. A lady standing nearby said, "Lee, ain't that Penny Man's son?" as she walked over to Donkey.

"Yeah," he replied. The woman smiled.

"He is so cute," she said as she dug into her purse and pulled out a dollar. She handed Donkey the money and instructed him to put it in his pocket.

Donkey had a second vision of himself at the age of nine. His mother had gone away for the weekend, and had left

Wayne Grind

Donkey and his kid brother at a neighbor's house. The babysitter's name was Sharon, and she was twenty-two years old. It was about nine-thirty one evening, and Donkey and his brother were fast asleep. Sharon came into the room where they slept, and woke him up. She took him into her bedroom. Once inside the bedroom, she locked the door and said, "You too good-looking not to know about this," as she opened up her long nightgown and let it drop to the floor. There, the babysitter stood naked in front of him.

Donkey's next vision was of a girl making wild and crazy remarks to him about how good he looked, saying, "Donkey baby, you look damn good."

Another lady said, "Lil' boy! My old man is away fighting for his country."

Another woman said, "Won't you let me take you home with me?"

"I'll suck your dick, baby, if you fuck as good as you look," said another. A random lady hopped out of a car and ran up to him, kissed him on his lips, and gave him a hundred dollar bill. Then she ran back to her car and left.

Another vision he had would not go away. It was the time he had an argument with a man named Quarter Horse. "Hate you mutha fuckas, that's, that's why I hate you pretty mutha fuckas, pretty, pretty, pretty mutha fuckas," and then he snapped out of his daydreams.
END FLASHBACKS.

Donkey turned to look at Bianca, and then he walked towards the hallway. He slipped a tape into his component set and pressed, "Play." He walked into the bedroom and cut off the television, slipped off his boxers, and got into the bed as the music began to play the song, "Between the Sheets" by the Isley Brothers. Bianca pulled off the burgundy satin nightgown and matching panties, tossed them onto the floor, and got into bed beside him. She laid back and opened her legs to where her cunt sat covered by a thick, black bush. It was drooling from the split because she was so horny and anxious for him to fuck her.

As he lay on top of her, he kissed her while placing one of his hands on her firm, erect breasts; he gripped it gently and started caressing it. He was teasing her before he fucked her. He started sucking her neck, nibbling on it and leaving a bruise, a mark of passion. He then licked down to her breast placing his mouth around one of them and began doing this thing with his tongue that sent this feeling through her body that most women love. She let out a soft moan, "Ummm," and then put her hand on the back of his head, locking his mouth around her nipple. The breast-sucking feeling that he gave her was irresistible. "Oh, bae!" she moaned, "Don't stop." After a minute or two, he came back up her body with his tongue to give her another kiss. He then grabbed his dick and slipped it into her pussy nice and slowly. She put one of her arms around his neck and the other one on his back while locking her legs around his waist. He started pushing his dick into her at a slow, lovemaking stride. "You know the spot," she whispered as he added this slight and undetected angle to his smooth stride. It was "a player's thing" he called it whenever they discussed their sex acts. She believed that the way he fucked her could be bought and sold on any street corner, but she knew the way he made love to her was priceless.

The clock read three-thirty-two in the morning. By five-eighteen in the morning, Donkey hadn't come yet. It had been two hours, and he was still sexing Bianca. Same strides, same position, and the part of the bed under her ass where she lie in ecstasy had gotten soaked from back-to-back orgasms. The moans and sounds which she let out stayed calm and slow as his routine stride remained smooth and easygoing. The Isley Brothers cassette had played all the way through and was on its third time around when he started feeling an orgasm coming on, so he raised himself up from the bed and started putting a bit of force behind his stride. Sweat ran from Bianca's face as she closed her eyes. The strides came stronger, the pace speeded up, and she began to scream as he pushed into her harder and harder, "Ohh! Ohh!"

Sweat dropped down from his face onto her breast as he looked down at his dick stabbing into her pussy. She continued to scream, "Ooh! Ooh! Bae! It's in my stomach!" But Donkey kept stroking, and she clawed into his back with her fingernails. He started thrusting even harder into her, and she screamed when he finally came inside of her. He continued to stroke until his dick was finish ejecting the complete package. When he had finished his major orgasm, he rolled over onto his back and lay next to Bianca. They both were exhausted, and then the alarm clock started ringing. He looked over at it and said, "Damn." It was five-thirty AM.

The next day at the car wash the whole gang was there just hanging around, doing a little bit of everything. Several different folks passed through since they had heard that Donkey had made it home. There was a barbecue grill set up in the parking lot, and a lot of sandwiches and appetizers were being served as well. Busty and Bo were sitting in front of the office, shooting the breeze. "Damn, Bee," said Bo. "That broad living that foul? Man, I can't believe it!"

Busty replied, "I can't see how she can live in that nasty-ass crib."

Some people just be trifling like that," Bo added. "Rats and shit hanging around. I would've left that mutha fucka, myself!"

Busty glanced over at Bo and he said, "I can't be trying to fuck something in no shit like that! I didn't fuck," said Busty. Bo looked at Busty curiously.

"What 'cha mean, you ain't fucked?" asked Bo. He gave Busty a strange look again.

Busty replied, "I could've fucked but I ain't want to." Then he just shrugged he shoulders.

"Why not?" Bo asked again.

Busty just hunched his shoulders again and said, "Cause I kind of like the broad, bro. I like her!"

Bo replied, "Man! You better leave that broad alone," he said, as he looked at the fifth cover where Big Bruce had soaked Champ up with a bucket of water and ran.

"Nigga, what makes you say that?" Busty asked.

But Bo was busy watching Champ run Big Bruce around the cars. "Ah! Them niggas gone crazy!" he said as he continued to look over at the fifth cover where they were.

Busty shook him to get his attention and asked, "Why do you think I should leave her alone?"

Bo turned around to look at Busty and said, "Man, a hoe like that ain't nothing but trouble," and he glanced over at Bruce and Champ again. "I went through the same shit with that bitch Kendra. I thought that she was the one," and he looked back at Busty as he continued, "It be all good until you make her more than a bitch to you. Man," he added, "Big Head Simon said that 'niggas been trying to turn hoes into women for years and ya can't change the B," and he turned to look Busty in his eyes. "They gotta want to change on their own."

Two weeks later at Shakespeare Park in Uptown, the majority of heroin pushers or users during that time were in, or in some way, affiliated with a tribe of Indians; Redd was one of them. During those days, there were only two major distributors of heroin in New Orleans: The Big Gate from Frisco, and WA 'Lee from Sky Town. The whole city was split up into two parts. They were Uptown and Downtown, and the major dealers made their money through the tribe's chief. Redd was affiliated with a tribe in an uptown area called The Wild Magnolia and the chief of the tribe was named Milton Pine, also known as Buffalo Chief. Buffalo Chief ran the uptown area known as the Third Ward.

One day Redd was asked to handle some serious business for Milton, The Buffalo Chief, who had a cousin that was robbed and killed a few months back. He had his hand in on Milton's drug organization and represented the tribe of The Wild Magnolia. After some time, Redd had learned that his cousin had been targeted to be assassinated by another tribe's chief named Crazy Horse, who was the chief of a tribe called the Gert Town Hunters. This was in an attempt to open up his territorial grounds. So Milton ordered a hit out on him, and the gang was going to take care of it.

"Aye, pothe way," the sound of tambourines, cheers, screams, and second-line music by the Rebirth Brass Band filled up the large grassy area of Hunter Field in Downtown. Champ popped a magazine into the butt of a forty-five caliber, and snapped a bullet into the chamber as he sat in an old Chevy station wagon' about a block away from the park. Busty sat across from me, and Bo sat in the back, alone.

"Champ, do you know him when you see him?" Bo asked.

Champ replied, "Naw! Just watch Redd and Sunshine." Then he stuffed an automatic forty-five Uzi into a handbag saying, "He can't hide."

Across the street from them in Redd's Cadillac, Redd said, "Here, Sunshine. Put this in your purse." Redd handed her the forty-five magnum. She grabbed it and placed it inside her purse.

Sunshine said, "Baby! You understand what you gotta do, huh?"

"Yeah, I got it," Bruce replied. "I need to make sure that they can see me at all times, and don't put the car in no hole," he added.

Then Sunshine asked Bae, "Where Silk and them at?"

"They somewhere around here," Redd replied as they got out of the car and walked toward the park. As they left, Bruce got out of the car and locked all the doors. Then he walked across the street to the station wagon. As he approached the station wagon, Champ, Busty, and Bo got out and walked toward the park behind Redd and Sunshine. They stood behind them about a half a block. Champ had his forty-five caliber stuffed in his waist. Bo had a three-fifty-seven magnum inside a Popeye's bag, and the Uzi was in the handbag carried by Busty.

On the corner of St. Bernard and North Daubigny, Silk, Donkey and Dusty sat in Silk's car watching the whole incident go down. Silk couldn't go because he was in a wheelchair. Dusty had just recently come home from the hospital and Redd said that Donkey would be easy to identify because of his scar, so they were just hanging around. As they sat in the car, Crazy Horse pulled up in the funeral home's parking lot at South Claiborne and Karce, "Look at that mutha fucka!" Silk said, as they watched him step out of a long white Continental.

"That's him?" asked Dusty, as another guy opened the trunk of the Continental.

"Yeah, that's him," Silk replied. Crazy Horse and another guy pulled out their Indian suits and started getting dressed in preparation for representing the tribe of the Gert Town Hunters. The other fella was Crazy Horse's younger brother Jerry, and their tribe's spy-boy. The spy-boy would always be the first to be scene before the chief and its tribe. Crazy

Wayne Grind

Horse slipped on a long, pretty breastplate that hung almost to his ankles; it had big, gorgeous, lime-green plumes hanging from it with a design made out on the breastplate. He reached into the truck to retrieve his sleeves and wings, and Silk saw something.

"He's strapped," he said as he turned around to look at Dusty. Then Silk said, "Go find Sunshine and tell her that the nigga is on his way, strapped with a vest." Donkey looked closer at Crazy Horse; he couldn't tell that he had on a vest or that he was strapped. Dusty got out of the car and walked across the field street to Hunter Field to search for Sunshine in the crowd. In the Field, Sunshine and Redd had found a spot not too deep in the crowd about twenty yards from the cotton candy stand. Champ. Bo, and Busty stood on the side of the stand about a yard or so away. They all were located closer to the St. Bernard and Claiborne Street side of the field. But Busty entered the field at the St. Bernard and Derbingy Street side and was searching for Sunshine and Redd.

A man screamed, "It was nineteen hundred and seventy eight. Spy-boy, don't go nowhere!"

When Champ first entered through Angola's gates, he heard, "Spy-boy, don't go nowhere!" It was Crazy Horse's younger brother Jerry, and he did his traditional stepping through the crowd to the sound of jingling tambourines.

The crowd opened up as he charged through for about ten steps to come to a halt. He then threw his hands in the air holding up his decorated hatched and tambourine as he cried out, "Big Chief Crazy Horse! Crazy Horse Big Chief!"

Then a loud scream came from behind him through the crowd, "Chief Almighty!" as the tribe of the Gert Town Hunters made their way through the crown and into Hunter's Field.

Once Crazy Horse was spotted, Redd and Sunshine started through the crowd headed toward the Gert Town, stepping ground. Bo said, "They moving!" So Bo, along with Champ and Busty, started walking behind them, lagging at a distance.

As Redd and Sunshine moved through the crowd, a guy walked up to Redd, "Woe, nah! Redd, what's up!" he shouted. There was so much noise being made that one had to speak very loudly.

Redd yelled, "What's up, CJ?"

"Ah, man! I'm just kicking it out hear with Lil' Boo," CJ replied as he and Redd turned to look at a tribe by the name of The Scene Boosters that was near them. "You know, he just started masking this year," CJ added as they watched a kid do some fancy steps representing his tribe.

The gang wasn't far behind. Busty looked through the crowd and saw Redd talking to CJ. He said, "That must be the tribe there?"

Bo looked over at the tribe. "Then which one of them is the chief?" he asked, and Champ began to look for the Scene Booster's chief.

He couldn't find him, and Champ said, "It ain't but six or seven of them." Busty turned to look at him, confused.

Sunshine looked back at the gang, and saw that they were looking for the chief of the tribe and turned back to Redd and said, "Bae! It's time to go!" He looked back at the gang and realized what was about to happen.

Sunshine walked away from CJ without saying anything, and he looked at Redd and mumbled, "And fuck you, too."

"Man, what the fuck they doing?" shouted Bo as they watched Redd and Sunshine walk away from CJ.

"That ain't the tribe!" replied Busty.

"What?" asked Champ.

"That ain't the tribe!" he shouted as they continued following Redd and Sunshine. On the other side of the field,

Dusty was still searching for Sunshine to tell them about the gun and the bulletproof vest.

Silk looked over onto the field and said, "Oh damn it!"

Donkey looked at him and asked, "What's up?"

Silk replied, "Redd's gonna be closer to the Gert Town Hunters!" And he wiped his forehead with his handkerchief. Dusty headed to the field, way over to the other side. Silk added, "He'll never get there in time!"

Donkey sighed, "Yeah," and looked over into the field. Redd and Sunshine neared the Gert Town Hunters tribe and Sunshine pulled out a camera from her purse. She started snapping pictures of the tribe.

They stood about ten yards or so away from Crazy Horse, and as the gang neared the tribe, Bo said, "That's the tribe!"

As Bo prepared to pull the pistol from the Popeye bag, Donkey spotted Champ not that far in the crowd and he got out of the car quickly. As he was about to head over to Champ, Silk asked him, "What are you doing?" Silk watched as he ran across St. Bernard Street onto the neutral ground, and then he noticed that he was trying to get Champ's attention as he waved his hands in the air. As the gang neared Crazy Horse's tribe, they split up. Champ was primarily on Crazy Horse's left side, but a tad behind him to be in a blind spot. Bo was on the opposite side, but positioned the same way. Busty on the other hand was directly in front of him, but camouflaged in the crowd about ten feet away.

The time had come. Busty and Bo looked at Sunshine, and she winked her eye. Then she turned around to kiss Redd. Champ looked through the crowd at St. Bernard Avenue and saw Big Bruce pull up in the station wagon to make sure they could get away, but then he saw Donkey standing on the neutral ground. He held the front of his shirt up with one hand and patted his chest with the other but Donkey couldn't figure out what he was saying.

It all happened so fast. Champ pulled out his pistol. Busty placed the handbag on the ground. Bo pulled the three-fifty-seven from the chicken bag. As the spy-boy of the tribe did his fancy stepping, he noticed Busty as he came upon them with the Uzi. The tambourine jingled, and the spy-boy's eyes widened as he shouted, "Gun!" and ran through the crowd.

When Crazy Horse heard the scream of his spy-boy, he quickly pulled out from under his shirt two forty-four magnums, one in each hand. Busty stepped through the crowd, aimed, and started letting loose at Crazy Horse's chest.

Crazy Horse fell to the ground while still pulling the trigger on the two guns and shooting into the crowd, and the stampede began. Busty frowned as he turned to shoot another Indian in Crazy Horse's tribe. The bullet ripped through his back and he fell to his death. Bo shot two more Indians from the tribe who tried to flee. He hit one in the back, and the other one in the head.

Champ walked over to Crazy Horse who was lying on the ground, and stuck the forty-five in his mouth and pulled the trigger shooting him five times. Then Bo ran up to him and snatched him by his shirt, "Enough! Let's go!" he yelled, and they all ran through the stampeding crowd toward the station wagon.

Running across St. Bernard Street toward the white Continental that was parked in the funeral home parking lot was Jerry, Crazy Horse's kid brother. Silk reached under the seat to retrieve a Colt forty-five, handed it to Donkey and said, "Go get him!"

Donkey grabbed the gun and said, "Cool," as he opened the door and got out of the car. Jerry opened the door to the Continental, got in and was fumbling with the keys in his hands before sticking them in the ignition. Once the keys were in the ignition, he looked to his left where he saw something out of the corner of his eye, and they widened as he looked down the barrel of the Colt forty-five. Donkey started letting loose, and Jerry's brains splattered all over the driver's side. His body slumped over on the front seat. Donkey ran back over to Silk's car and saw the rest of the gang spin away down St. Bernard Street in the station wagon. He got in the car, and he and Silk pulled off. After the shooting, Dusty caught up with Redd and Sunshine and came home with them. Donkey couldn't hang around after killing Jerry, so he had to leave.

The war was on. In the heroin game, a man with money was a man with power, and a man with a lot of power was Big Gate. He ran half of the heroin being sold in New Orleans from his San Francisco Mansion. Crazy Horse was one of Big Gate's territorial lords in the Crescent City, combined with the other tribe chiefs; they formed a notorious heroin organization that pulled in nearly a million dollars a day. This was more than sixty-five percent of the money being made in New Orleans off of heroin. The only thing that kept Big Gate from controlling the city's entire heroin market was a guy named WA 'Lee who was from Chicago, but his share of the market was much smaller. He strained about four hundred grand on his best of days which was about thirty-seven percent of the market, but his organization was even smaller than Big Gate's with only four tribe chiefs in the family. Big Gate's family doubled WA 'Lee's family at least twice, but after all of the comparisons, they both were equal in power.

The four tribe chiefs in WA 'Lee's organization were Buffalo Chief of The Wild Magnolia, Kyle Evans of The Mohawk Hunters of Algiers, Dollar Bill of The Flaming Arrows, and Toddy Montana of The Yellow Pocahontas. After learning of the assassination of Crazy Horse at Hunters Field, everybody expected retaliation in a hurry, but it didn't come until a week later.

The Mohawk Hunters were stepping down Whitney Avenue one week before Super Sunday. Kyle Evans was their stepping chief and he was marked to be assassinated by The House who was the chief of a tribe called The Carrolton Hunters, and the most respected of all chiefs. As Kyle Evans and the Mohawk Hunters second-lined down Whitney Avenue toward Newton Street, the sound of the Pin Striped Brass Band followed, "Do your thang, bey!" a lady yelled from behind Kyle as he held his staff in the air. Turning around to look at his wife, he just smiled and continued to step. Just before Newton Street, the second line passed two guys who sat on the hood of a Mark Five, and Kyle noticed them but he didn't know them from anywhere. They stared at Kyle as he passed by them, but he didn't think anything of it. He thought that he would keep an eye on them from time to time. Kyle's wife stared at the two guys also, and she to found something strange about the two guys on the hood of the Lincoln. The second line made it to the intersection of Whitney and Newton Street, and The Mohawk Tribe stopped in the middle of the street and bucked.

Kyle cried out to the crowd, "Aye, Aye, Aye!" and the crowd shouted back, "Aye! Pothe way!" Then when a gap opened up in the crowd and Kyle was able to look down the street at the Lincoln, it was gone. He began to get wary, and as he continued to do his fancy stepping he looked at his wife and noticed that she had an expression on her face that was full of curiosity. This made Kyle paranoid. As he stepped, he tried to place the two guys but not one of them was in the crowd.

"Get down, Kyle!" someone yelled.

"Duck, Kyle!" said another.

But Kyle kept stepping. He felt nobody but his wife could tell that something was wrong. As he continued to step he looked through the crowd, and a gap opened up again. He saw the Mark Five heading down Whitney toward the Fisher Projects so he started smiling. Everything was alright, and then he thought about his wife so he turned around to give her a nice big smile when it hit him. One shot was fired into his forehead and his brains splattered into the face of the tribe's spy-boy as Kyle fell to the ground. A lady yelled, "That bitch shot Kyle," as his wife dropped a forty-five magnum to the ground beside his body. Suddenly, a crowd of people bomb-rushed her, shouting, "Whoop that bitch!" and "Kill that hoe!" Then people started kicking and stomping her. They stabbed and spit on her, and punched her repeatedly.

Two days later, Busty asked Coniece, "How come you be moving from place to place?" as they rode in his Cadillac on the Interstate headed east.

She replied, "I just don't be wanting to stay in the same place," as she stared out the window.

"So who is this mutha fucka to you?" shouted Busty, and Coniece was startled at how he spoke to her.

She replied, "How come you asking me all these damn questions?" She turned to look at him.

"Bitch, cause you in my mutha fucking shit, that why!" he yelled as he began to get more pissed off. He pulled to the side of the Interstate and brought the car to a stop. "Get the fuck out!" he said, and she just looked at him. "Bitch, get out!" he yelled even louder, and she opened the car door. He reached toward the back seat to grab a few pieces of chicken that he had left from Popeye's, and tossed them out the passenger door saying, "Trifling bitch, a player can't be nice to yo ass." She looked back at him and he added, "Nigga been trying to make a women out of bitches like you for years, but a bitch gon' always be a bitch. Now close the mutha fucking door!" She closed the door, and he pulled off, leaving her standing on the Interstate at one thirty in the morning about a mile from the nearest exit. She watched Busty as he raced up the Interstate and tears started rolling down her face because she never thought a man could be so cruel.

One day Champ got a call at his house from Principal Hanes. He said, "Wayne! When do you plan on returning to school? You have turned me into a laughing stock over here!" He added, "You haven't been to school in over a month now, and Mr. Walker has come and asked me about you every single day."

Champ replied, "Mr. Hanes, I have been having a few problems and shit."

"Like what?" he asked.

"You know, with Corey in a coma and my people getting shot up. It's been kind of hectic," he said.

Then Mr. Hanes said, "Wayne, listen. During all of your trials and tribulations, you should practice on learning how to maintain, or your adversaries will always stay on top of you," he said. "Wayne, a soldier is at his best in his worse times, so what'cha gon' do?" he asked.

Champ thought for a moment. "Man, I don't know. I'll have to think about it a bit more," he mumbled.

"Well, that's good enough for me. You can have the whole weekend to think about it!" he shouted. "And best wishes to Corey for a speedy recovery," he added, and hung up. Champ always did find Mr. Hanes kind of cool, but then realized that he really didn't give a fuck.

His podna Corey was still in a coma fighting for his life after they both were ganged by some player haters beating one day after school. Every other day or so Champ would pass by the hospital and check on him, and just in case something happened to him, he left his home number written on a piece of paper and taped it to the wall just over his bed. Champ had really been missing him lately. Hell, he had been in a coma for thirty-seven days now, and even the rest of the gang had been wondering how he was doing.

Sand claimed that Champ hadn't been myself since he got hurt. He was sorely missed.

Big Gate's organization was furious after Crazy Horse was killed, especially after the murder of Kyle Evans on an Algiers intersection in front of a crowd of people at a Second Line. A string of notorious killings followed; killings which were brought upon two of the only three members of WA 'Lee's Crescent City organization who were left. On a Friday evening at about three o'clock, Redd sat in Charlie's Barber Shop getting a trim when they looked at a special bulletin on the television. It was broadcasting the bloody homicide of Dollar Bill, who was the Chief of The Flaming Arrows. His long, black Continental was surrounded by five masked men in the parking lot of a Schwegman Supermarket as he sat in his car. The bullets ripped through his car and riddled his body. He was dead when the first policeman found him slumped over his steering wheel. Rudy Montana had been missing for several days when a waste worker for the city dump discovered his decomposed body in a pile of garbage as a garbage truck unloaded into a landfill. A large portion of the back of his skull was missing and he had been dead for at least five days. The odor was unimaginable. The only thing that kept Rudy from being stuffed into the morgue with a John Doe toe tag was the tattoo he had on his left shoulder that read "Big Chief Rudy Montana" in old English letters.

Holly's baby daddy Rueben who was in the Angola State Penitentiary for first-degree murder was finishing up his daily workout on the weight pile with a few other guys. "Come on, nigga!" a guy yelled as he stood over Rueben, who was straining to push up two-forty on the crossbar one final time. "Rueben, you ain't shit!" The guy yelled as Rueben strained it up to the top.

Rueben set the crossbar down and sat on the bench,

exhaled deeply, and said, "Fuck you, Lake Charles," as they laughed.

Then Lake Charles added, "Tomorrow we can start on the three hundred if ya want."

Rueben replied, "Cool."

Lake Charles picked up his shirt off the ground and said, "Well, I'ma holla at cha tomorrow," as he walked away.

"After chow!" Rueben yelled, "We gon' get started kind of early."

Lake Charles waved his hand and kept walking. Rueben sat on the bench and relaxed for a while, and another guy walked up. "Woah, Rueben. What's up?" the guy shouted as he approached.

Rueben gave the guy a handshake while saying, "I heard you was back, nigga. You just don't agree with society, huh?" Rueben asked.

The guy stooped down next to the bench and said, "Man, you know how shit be happening."

Rueben glanced over at some prisoners playing basketball. "Yeah, Ben, I know," he mumbled, and then he reached inside his boot and pulled out a pack of Camel cigarettes. "Want a bump?" he asked, and Ben reached out to pull a cigarette from the pack. Rueben pulled out another cigarette and stuck it in his mouth, and then lit his and Ben's cigarettes. "So, what's up nigga?" he asked. "I heard you and old Buddy was running pretty hard out there, huh?"

Ben replied, "Yeah, but since I been down, he been doing most of my running."

"Oh, yeah," said Rueben.

Ben added, "This nigga Truck was fucking Buddy's cousin, and he'd peel us out a few grand to push up Frisco and back with a Lil' something. Hell, I flipped a new Riviera and a pad."

Rueben took a pull off of the cigarette, exhaled and said, "So what chu got popped for?"

Ben replied, "Law pulled my shit over on Franklin and Galvez, and caught me with a half a package of thirty-fives and a set-up."

"What they gave ya?" asked Rueben.

Ben answered, "Well, my lawyer got me ten without the bill, so I took it and ran. Hell, I'ma four-time loser. I was looking at twenty-five with the "L" from a mile away with a pair of sunshades on," to which they both had a bittersweet laugh.

"Yeah, my nigga!" Reuben said, "You most definitely saw twenty-to-life." He flicked the cigarette butt onto the ground. "So old Buddy gon' run this nickel down for ya, huh?"

Ben tossed his cigarette to the ground and replied, "Yeah, him and my Lil' settler gon' josh me, but right now, that nigga gone though."

"Gone where?" asked Rueben.

"Up to Frisco," replied Ben, and Rueben started laughing.

"Man, Buddy must be crazy to be riding back down with that shit!" stated Rueben.

"Naw!" Ben shouted, "He gon' bus it back."

Then Reuben added, "You know the troopers be stopping everything, especially when you be coming through Texas."

Ben added, "Yeah, they be hot coming through Dallas, too." They sat and watched the other prisoners play basketball. Ben said, "But when he comes in, Imma give him a call at the motel and shit, ya know? Gonna let 'em know I made it to the yard."

Rueben replied, "That nigga Ben be playing them quick stops to keep law from running in on him, huh!"

"Yeah!" confirmed Ben. "When he hit Sunday, he just gon' drop in at the Howard until Truck come and get him."

"Well, shit. He laid back!" said Rueben. "I don't blame him." Then the horn sounded off for the prisoners to make their way to their camps, so the two of them got up off of the weight bench and left the yard.

Back in New Orleans, life continued. Since the deaths of Kyle Evans, Dollar Bill, and Rudy Montana, Milton's business had been very low-key. It was obvious that if he would ever be caught slipping he'd be the next tribal chief to be assassinated, so he made all of his moves during the dark hours and very carefully. One Saturday night, Milton pulled into the car wash in this big, shiny green Jeep Wagoneer. He pulled the jeep through the lot and parked it behind Redd's Fleetwood, who had just arrived about twenty minutes earlier. Milton, along with two other guys hopped out of the jeep and walked across the lot toward the office. They never once looked over toward the fourth cover where Champ, Busty, and Donkey stood armed with assault rifles in case of danger. As they headed to the office, one guy who looked as if he had a little age on him said, "Milton! Man, how good do you know this mutha fucka?"

The other younger fella who was maybe eighteen or so added, "That's on the real, Unk. Because I passed around here before," said the boy as he looked around the car wash lot. "And this mutha fucka used to be packed around this time, Unk, but now I don't trust this shit."

Milton stopped just before he got to the door of the office. He looked at both of them and said, "Y'all look here. Y'all should know by now that I handpick my people."

"Just like Kyle picked his bitch!" shouted the younger guy abruptly. "Now Unk," he added as anger and frustration showed on his face, "You know damn well that don't mean shit when you fucking with House. I understand where you coming from, Unk!" he shouted, "But you gotta understand me, too."

Milton looked at the youngster, and he knew the kid meant well. He was only trying to remind Milton of what type of people they were beefing with. House was one of the most scandalous. Milton replied, "Well alright," as he nodded his head slightly, "But I'ma tell you like this," he added. "I respect the way you looking at everything in this situation, but you gotta trust me on this one, alright?"

The older guy nodded his head, and the younger one mumbled, "Yeah, it's cool."

When they stepped up to the door of the office, Milton knocked. Redd walked to the door and opened it without answering because he knew that Milton was coming. He knew this because they had talked on the phone before Milton arrived. Once they were in the office, Redd closed the door and the kid that was with him looked at everybody in the office with a suspicious look. Silk sat behind the desk in his wheelchair, Dusty and Bruce played poker on the desktop, and Bo sat on a high stool across the room next to the water cooler.

Milton walked over to the desk and gave Silk a firm handshake. "What's been going on, Silky?" he asked.

"Ah, it ain't 'bout nothing," replied Silk as he looked over at the two guys who had come with Milton. They stood still by the front door, like soldiers. Silk looked at the kid and asked, "What's your name, Lil' man?"

The kid waited for a few minutes in silence and then turned to look at Bo, who in turn was looking at him, and so was everybody else in the office. The kid mumbled something under his breath that was not easily understood, "Man, why this nigga watching me and shit?" Milton turned to look at him, and Bo looked over at Milton.

Milton saw that the kid was staring at Bo, and what unfolded next all happened so quickly. The kid and Bo went for their pistols, which sat at their waist. The other fella who was with Milton went for his pistol, and the sounds of hammers being cocked on the pistols filled the office. Silk's eyes widened as it all happened before him: the old guy had a forty-five revolver aimed at Redd; the kid held a Beretta m9 aimed at Bo; Bo had one hand around Milton's neck, and a forty-five in his other hand pressed against the back of his head. "*Man, what the fuck!*" shouted Silk as he rested back in his wheelchair. Bruce and Dusty also wondered what was going on.

Milton said, "Neil, put the damn gun down!"

"Not until we find out what the fuck's going on!" replied the older guy. Outside in the parking lot under the fourth cover, the boys were smoking a reefer as they stood watch outside and hustled.

"Man, I told yo ass the other day that we don't need no carjack," Busty said to a dope fiend who was trying to get off some carjacks.

"But Bizzy Man, I just brought you that color TV the other day," replied the dope fiend. "You know when I get them silks and shit, I'ma take care of ya. Do something for me, bra. You know I'ma hustler."

"Busty, give him a few balloons," said Donkey as he puffed on the reefer. "Ray know he can't duck us."

Inside the office, Silk said, "Bo. Put the gun down." Silk tried to keep his cool but wanted to sound like he meant business, too.

"What?" asked Bo as he stared into Silk's eyes.

Silk added, "We gotta start somewhere, Bo," and he patted his hand on the desktop. "Now put it down!" he said again. "Everything gon' be alright." Silk spoke to Bo in a very calm manner, but with authority. However, Silk saw in Bo's eyes that he didn't want to put his forty-five down.

Bruce added, "Put it down, bra. Please!" Bo glanced at Bruce and then back at Silk. Then Bo closed his eyes while slowly lowering his head to look at the ground. Silk's eyes widened as he realized the next second could be critical.

But then it happened. Very slowly, Bo lowered the pistol down from Milton's head. He then sat down on the desktop. Milton exhaled, deeply relieved. Bo opened his eyes to look directly at Silk. Silk's eyes were full of fire. Bo let Milton go, and then he turned and walked into the back room of the office. All eyes were on Bo, yet the room stayed silent. Once Bo had walked out of the room, the kid and the older guy had put their weapons back under their shirts. Redd walked over to sit on the corner of the desk and Silk said, "Now! Let's start this over again," as he looked at the kid. "What's your name, Lil' man?"

The kid grinned and replied, "Neil."

"Well, look here!" Slim said. "I'm Silky Slim, and I think I'ma like having you around, Neil," as he looked at the kid with quite a sneaky grin.

Outside of the office, Champ said, "Donkey," as he held a stack of bills in his hand, "Snatch about nine of them out the back for this nigga right here." The dope fiend looked on eagerly, as Champ walked out the back of the fourth cover to retrieve nine balloons from the stash.

After Donkey organized the bills to be face up, he began to count the money. As he counted, he said under his breath, "Ninety-eight, ninety-nine, three – damn stones!" he yelled as he continued to recount the money.

Busty started laughing. "I bet that nigga came with a hundred and fifty ones, huh?" added Busty, when Champ returned from the stash and handed nine balloons to the dope fiend.

The druggie started walking off while asking Donkey, "That's it? Huh, Lil' daddy?"

"Yeah, yeah," replied Donkey, "This three-eighteen stone; it's cool!" Just like that, the dope fiend was gone. Donkey handed the money out to Champ, who gave Donkey a very strange look.

"What?" Champ asked, and Busty started laughing.

"Put this back there!" Donkey shouted. Then Champ started laughing again; he laughed until tears ran down Busty's face. Busty and Champ were dying of laughter.

Donkey realized that the joke was on him and said, "Man, mutha fuck y'all," and started back to the stash. In the back of the corner, there was a large brown paper bag sitting next to a tin, fifty-gallon garbage can. Donkey lifted up the lid of the garbage can and there was an enormous amount of U.S. currency piled up halfway to the top. He tossed the small stack of bills from his hand into the can, and placed the lid back on it. Then he reached down to open the brown bag. Inside the bag, there were about seven whole packages of heroin. "Damn," said Donkey too quietly, "We gon' have to get some more," he added as he closed the bag and left.

Back in the office, Redd stated, "That fat mutha fuckas tryin' to take over everything. That's what he's up to." Redd sat on the edge of the desk, while Milton sat on a chair in front of the desk with his legs cocked up on the edge. Neil and Bo were in the back room shooting the breeze. Silk figured after what had taken place earlier, maybe those two should try to get to know each other better.

"Full House," said the older guy who was playing cards on the desktop. He had come with Milton. After everything had cooled off, he had ended up playing poker with Dusty and Bruce.

"I fold," Bruce said, as he threw his hand in.

The older guy looked at Bruce and said, "Well, what'cha got, Lil' nigga?"

Dusty smiled as he laid his hand down and said, "Royal Flush."

"Ah, shit," sighed the older guy. "You Lil' niggas got more luck than sense," he said as Dusty drew the pot toward him. Silk, Redd, and Milton were trying to figure out what their next move would be because Milton was sure there was a gang of killers out looking high and low for him.

Silk said, "What you think, Redd?"

Redd replied, "Man, I don't know, Slim! It's only so many of us." He added, "If we set up shop in the front of town, that ain't gon' do shit but turn it into a killing field."

"Well. We gotta do something, and soon," Slim said.

"I say we go around there and leave a blood bath whenever those mutha fuckas fuck up," suggested Dusty as he played poker.

Slim and Redd weren't playing any attention to what Dusty had said, but Milton was listening and said, "Hold up. Hold up!" He was trying to get Slim and Redd's attention. "Lil' daddy, what'cha just say?" he asked.

Dusty turned to look at Milton and replied, "That nigga Truck's killing all of the chiefs that work for WA 'Lee, right?" Silk looked at him, puzzled. "So without the chiefs, WA 'Lee can't make any money, right?" continued Milton.

"Yeah, go on!" Redd replied, and Dusty continued.

"Then we kill all his chiefs and their workers," he added. "Then the strongest man gon' win," and Silk and Redd both looked at Milton and he hunched his shoulders.

That night when Champ got home, Sand told him that Holly had been calling for him back-to-back. When he called her back, she asked, "Champ, have you and Bo been sending Rueben money or something?"

"No, we ain't been sending him nothing. Why?" Champ asked.

Sand replied, "Because he said that he wants to talk to you about something. I had him on a three-way, but I couldn't catch up with yo ass," she replied.

"Alright then, I'ma hang around the crib until about eleven. If he calls tomorrow just holla at me," he told Sand.

"Champ, you better be home because that boy says that it's important!" she yelled.

"I'ma be home," Champ replied. "Now, go ahead, girl! Because a nigga 'bout to do his thang," He added.

Then she said, "Champ, you so nasty!" She hung up the phone.

The next day when Champ talked to Rueben, he said that he had some info on a heist for a nice bit of stash. Ruben said that whatever they licked for on the heist, he was positively sure it would be a kilo or more. Champ couldn't refuse, because a kilo of heroin was worth mad cash on the streets.

Ruben also told Champ that a chump was pulling in from San Francisco on Sunday night and was going to lay low at the Howard Johnson Hotel until he made the drop. It would be hit and miss because the pickup probably wouldn't be far behind. The old problem they had was they didn't know what the chump looked like. They couldn't tell Silk about the heist because they knew that he didn't approve of jacking. Instead, Champ, Donkey, Busty and Bruce went and had a plan of their own.

Big Bruce would always be coming up with some type of plan when it was time to do something, and Donkey said that he had been watching too many episodes of *Mission Impossible*. The plan he had was really as simple as one, two, three, since nobody knew what the guy looked like. So they would depend on their street instincts and if they were lucky, it would all be good. If they were not, they would simply miss him.

The bus that Rueben said the guy would touch down on pulled up to the Greyhound Bus Station at nine thirty-five. Herman (Donkey's cousin) had hooked them up with two hot cars. Champ and Busty sat in the parking lot of the station in a hot Buick La Sabre; there wasn't any need for major heat so they just took handguns along. Donkey sat on the hood of a hot Monte Carlo in front of the terminal, as if he had come to pick somebody up; he had a forty-five on the passenger seat. Big Bruce was inside playing an arcade game, since he came up with the idea. They all suggested that he do the hard part of identifying their man.

The nine thirty-five passengers on the bus who had arrived from San Francisco had exited the bus and entered the terminal. Bruce watched them very carefully; the young, white girl with the red suitcase; the soldier; the Hispanic couple; the two old ladies; etc. But then one guy caught Bruce's attention. He had on a dark gray, double-breasted suit, a black tie, black patent leather shoes, and he carried a small suitcase in one hand and a black Beaver skin Dobbs' hat in the other. He had a nugget ring and watch on his left hand. His face was pale. He appeared to be a little paranoid, or at least not relaxed, but his stride was too professional. He walked past Bruce and exited the terminal. As he waved for a taxi, Bruce exited the terminal and stood just a few feet on the side of him. Bruce then looked at Donkey and he turned and walked around his car and got in. A taxi pulled up, and the guy started towards it. Big Bruce rushed to another taxi behind the first one, and so did another guy. "Sorry, kid," the guy said as he grabbed the taxi's back door handle. "My cab," he reiterated. Bruce looked this guy over. He had on a black-and-white, thin-striped Casino shirt, a pair of black slacks, and a pair of brown gator skin shoes. "Come on, kid. Get outta here!" he said loudly, as he opened the door and got in the taxi.

Bruce then rushed to the next taxi that was in line, got in and told the driver to follow the taxi that the first man had entered. He kind of barked the orders as he got in and closed the door. Once seeing him get into the taxi through his rear-view mirror, Champ pulled out in the La Sabre in front of all three taxis. As they pulled off, Donkey pulled up beside the taxi that Bruce was riding.

At the hotel, Champ and Busty had gotten out of the La Sabre and were just entering the hotel's lobby when the first taxi pulled into the lobby tunnel. The guy in the suit got out, tipped the driver, and walked into the lobby. The second guy with the gator skin shoes pulled up in his taxi, and he, too, got out and tipped the driver. Then he went into the lobby.

The taxi that Bruce was in didn't enter the tunnel, because he had gotten out on a side street and walked around to the lobby. Donkey parked the Monte Carlo out front on Howard Avenue (so that he could see into the lobby), and just waited. Inside the lobby, Busty took a seat and pretended as if he was reading a magazine. Champ stood at the counter putting his mack down on this young female desk clerk. The first guy in the suit paid for a suite in room 412 and at another desk, the guy with the gator skin shoes paid for a single room in 209. The first guy walked through the room toward to the elevator, pressed the up button, and waited.

Then the female clerk shouted, "Excuse me, Sir. Excuse me!" as she looked over at Bruce who had walked into the lobby and walked straight past the desk toward the elevator. The elevator door opened, the first guy stepped in and held the door for the second guy, who in turn held the door for Bruce. "Security! Security!" the female clerk shouted as Busty walked up to her. He pulled his pistol out and smacked her across the face, knocking her unconscious.

"Bitch, don't move," Busty said as he pointed the pistol at the other male desk clerks.

"We ain't moving," one of them whispered as they both held their hands in the air.

When Bruce made it to the elevator, he had his pistol in his hand, and he said, "Alright, I want ya suit cases!" as he stood with his foot in the elevator door and waved the pistol in their faces. The guy in the suit slowly sat his suitcase down in front of Bruce and stepped back. As Champ walked up, the second guy stared at Bruce as if knowing his face from somewhere, and he didn't want to give up his suitcase. Bruce looked down at the suitcase then back into the guy's eyes. "Just pass me the suitcase," he said, but the guy didn't budge. "You gon' die for that, mutha fucka?" Bruce shouted.

"Fuck you!" the guy shouted.

"Ah-ah, nigga! Fuck you!" Bruce shouted again, and then he opened fire into the elevator. The first guy watched the second guy's bloody body fall in the corner of the elevator, and Bruce reached in and grabbed the suitcase. Then they ran out of the hotel lobby. Donkey pulled up in the Monte Carlo, and they took off.

After pulling the heist, they pushed to Holly's house to search the bags. "Man, they got clothes in this shit," shouted Busty as he looked through the things from the first guy's suitcase which he had dumped on the bed.

"Y'all was robbing people for their suitcase!" yelled Holly as she watched Busty search the suitcase. The only thing of any value was a nice camera and a wallet which contained a gold clip and eighteen hundred dollars. Busty slipped the money clip off the roll of money and tossed the money across the room over to Holly.

Bruce then grabbed the second guy's suitcase and opened it. It was full with clothes that were neatly stacked in place. "More clothes," he said as he started throwing the clothes out of the suitcase and tossing them on the bed.

After he had thrown all of the clothes onto the bed, he said, "Holy Shit!" He stared into the suitcase. His eyes had gotten so big, you would have thought he had seen a ghost.

Everybody looked into the suitcase. "Damn," Donkey said. Bruce reached into the suitcase and held up a whole kilo of heroin.

"Man!" Busty sighed. "So this is what a kilo looks like?" he asked as he tossed it on the bed. Then he reached back into the suitcase and started pulling out more heroin and tossing it onto the bed. There were four kilos in all. Busty said, "That's enough to supply the whole city for the rest of the month! Shidd!"

Donkey added, "More like six months."

Bruce picked up the rest of the heroin and said, "It's only one way to find out," and then he looked at them all and added, "We gotta find out how good it is!"

At the car wash, Bo and Silk was in the office just chilling. Bo was on the phone with his girlfriend Minnie. "Girl, I ain't getting married!" and he started laughing.

"Oh! You wouldn't marry me, nigga?" Minnie asked.

He replied, "I ain't saying that I wouldn't marry you," and he added, "But, um..."

"But um, what?" she asked.

"Let me talk!" yelled Bo, and he started laughing again.

"No, mutha fucka! You don't have to put no ring on my finger," said Minnie. "But when I tell Jane Lee not to let your ass in here," she added.

Bo smacked his lips, "So we gon' go by my house?" he shouted.

"I ain't goin' by your house," replied Minnie.

"Why not?" Bo asked, and then she giggled.

Finally Minnie said, "We ain't doing it no more."

Bo yelled, "I'ma show yo ass!"

Minnie chuckled some more, "Oh, now you mad?" she said, and all of a sudden he heard a horn blowing from outside.

Silk said, "Bo, see who that is!"

Bo stood up and told her, "Look, I'ma call you back."

Minnie yelled, "Don't call over here again." Then she hung up the phone and he smiled as he hung up.

Bo said, "Yeah! I'ma get her ass," and walked to the door.

When Bo reached the front door, he looked out and heard someone say, "Come on, player. Let's ride!" The two guys who were with Milton the other night were there in the same big green Jeep Wagoneer, so he closed the door and walked over to the jeep.

"What's up, bro?" Neil asked as he sat in the front seat of the jeep.

"I'm just chilling," Bo replied as he reached inside the jeep and gave them both a handshake.

"You in there letting that Lil' nigga cheat on ya with them cards, huh?" said the older guy.

Bo was humored and laughed. He said, "Naw! That Lil' nigga is around the corner fucking with them Lil' hoes and shit."

"But what y'all up to? Man, I was thinking about riding up to Gert Town and killin' a few of them niggas, "Neil replied.

Bo asked, "What y'all got like that?" Then he looked in the back seat.

"Just a couple of K's," Neil replied.

Bo looked at him and said, "Hold on, I be right out." When Bo returned to the jeep he got in and they left. They were on their way to Gert Town with two AK-47's and a couple of handguns.

As they rode down Washington Avenue, Neil lit up a reefer and took a few pulls off of it, and passed it back to Bo. Neil said, "Freddie, if we wouldn't have fell on that charge," and then he exhaled a thick cloud of smoke, "That fat mutha fucka House would've been X'd out."

Freddie replied, "Believe that," as he took a right turn on South Broad by Popeye's.

"Man, where you going?" Neil asked as they coasted up Broad Street.

"Neil, I'm just gon' run in there and holla at her and gon' come right out!" replied Freddie, and he sat back in his seat, a bit upset.

As Bo passed the reefer back up to him he said, "Nigga, you a mutha fucking lie!" As they came up to Erato Street, he took a right turn and headed down Erato into the Zane City area.

Freddie drove up Erato to Gayoso Street, where there were three fellas hanging on the corner. The lime tint on the jeep had the three guys playing close attention to them as it took a right turn onto Gayoso. He drove up Gayoso little bit more than a half of block, and parked in front of a brick four-plex. He had a girlfriend that lived in one of the upstairs units. From the jeep, he looked up to see that the light was on in her bedroom. He grabbed the handle and opened the door. That's when Neil said, "Gimme my keys, bra, cause if you gon' be long, I'm riding out on the real!"

Freddie replied, "I ain't gon' be long." He tossed the keys to Neil and closed the door, then headed up to his girlfriend's crib.

When he left, Neil said, "Man, I don't know why he even fuck with that bitch," as he watched him walk up the front stairs and knock on the door. "He can't even fuck her unless he buys that bitch something," he added and he turned around.

Then he noticed Bo looking back toward the corner at the three guys. "What's up, man?" he asked Bo.

Bo replied, "I know one of them niggas!"

"Which one?" Neil asked.

"That kid Damien along with Do Dirty and another fella was hanging out on the corner from his mother's house," said Bo.

Down the street, one of the fellas said, "Say Dee. That's the nigga that fell on that charge with Neil that time when yo cousin got shot up."

Damien replied, "No that ain't."

"I'm telling ya, Dee," as he looked down toward the jeep. "Because that nigga got that Lil' primed up Regal, remember? I'm telling ya, Dee," the guy said. "I was by Bay Bay's house one day and he brought ya girl over there to get her hair fixed," he added. "You know her and Bay Bay is kin."

Damien just stared down the block toward the jeep and said, "You know where that Regal be at?"

The other guy said, "On Willow Street across from Edward P. Harney," and then he added, "Cause when I be going by Lynn, I be seeing this red broad driving it sometimes. I think that's his sister or something."

Back in the jeep, Freddie opened the door, grabbed his pistol from under the driver's seat, and closed the door. Then he went back up to the apartment. "Man, what's this nigga going to do?" shouted Neil, as he and Bo got out of the jeep and went up to the apartment behind him.

On the corner, Damien and the other fella had started walking toward his mother's house after seeing Neil hop out of the jeep. Damien had a grudge against him from something that had happened nearly a year ago.

FLASHBACK:

Neil and his cousin Ron were riding up Simon Bolivar Boulevard to La Salle on November 14th of the previous year. "Yeah, Neil!" Ron said as he drove his candy-apple red Park Avenue. "Like I was trying to tell your uncle, he been too good to me for me to be pulling off some shit like that, bra."

"For real," replied Neil, "But you know how Unk can be tripping."

Ron glanced over at Neil, and then back at the road and said, "I don't even know why Milton left all that shit by Mae Mae's house anyway." And Neil just looked at him. Ron continued, "He know that bitch be mainstreaming."

Neil turned to look out the window, then said, "I was telling Unk that shit," as Ron made a right turn onto Washington Avenue. "He claims that for seventeen years of knowing her, she ain't never stole from him," Neil said. Ron drove down Washington, a block from Ferret Street, and took a left on Magnolia at 17th street onto Ferret. He pulled over, parked, and turned off the ignition.

"Say Neil, man," Ron said, "Want 'cha talk to Milton for me!"

"Man! Don't trip on that shit," replied Neil as he opened the passenger door. Then he said, "Oh yeah! I'ma bring you three of 'em down instead of two, and you just owe me a grand."

Ron replied, "Alright." Neil closed the door and left. Ron thought he had patched everything up between him and Neil, and he was even gladder that he had gotten his connection back more than anything else.

Ron had waited in the car for Neil to return from this apartment where Milton kept his heroin. Neil and Freddie were in the hallway and Neil pulled a three fifty seven from his waist and said, "Man, just slip on the mutha fucking mask," and he pulled a mask down over his face. Freddie pulled a ski mask down over his face, too, and cocked back the sawed-off shotgun when somebody said, "Oh, Neil." They looked to the end of the hallway and saw that it was Ron. For some reason, Ron did not think that it was safe for him to be sitting inside a car at one o'clock in the morning in the projects. Neil and Ron looked in each other's eyes for a quick second, and then Ron sprinted away off the porch, around the building and onto the courtyard. Neil and Freddie were right behind.

Ron was running for his life, about twenty feet ahead of Neil. He wasn't very far away, but there was always something blocking Neil from getting a clear shot. Freddie trailed behind Neil about ten feet away as Neil ran through the courtyard. Then Neil took the only shot at Ron that he thought was possible, and Ron fell to the ground.

To this day, Neil never knew that the first shot he had fired never hit Ron. Ron had been running very fast, but was so scared that as soon as the shot was fired, he fell face down to the ground. As they ran up to him, he made an effort to get up. That is when Neil unloaded the last five shots from the 357mg into Ron's back. The police sirens started screaming from a distance as he shot.

Then Freddie caught up. He stood over Ron with his shotgun and shot him three more times. They fled away through the courtyard as a couple of police cars approached. END FLASHBACK.

At the house in Zane City where Freddie's girlfriend was, Freddie yelled as Neil and Bo tried to calm him down, "What the fuck that nigga doing here anyway?" Freddie continued to shout as Neil tried to pull him out of the door.

"Bitch, we about to fuck" the female yelled.

"Man, come on!" shouted Neil as he pulled him down the stairs.

"Man, I'ma stomp that bitch," Freddie said as he walked over to the jeep and opened the door, getting in. Neil looked to the apartment at Bo, who was trying to apologize to the broad for Freddie's behavior.

"Come on, Bo," he yelled. "Let's get the fuck out of here!" Then Bo came down the stairs and got in the jeep.

Bo looked at Neil and said, "Man, ya girl cold as a mutha fucka."

Neil said, "I been told 'em 'bout that bitch," as he opened the front door of the jeep. He grabbed his pistol from his waist so that he could sit down comfortably, and as he did, Bo opened the back door and got in.

Inside the jeep Freddie yelled, "Man, where the fucking keys at?" as he and Neil turned to look at each other.

Neil replied, "Man, she pissed you off."

"Not me," Freddie replied as Neil handed him the keys. As Freddie searched for the ignition key, Neil glanced through the rearview mirror, because he thought that he saw something.

Freddie mumbled, "I'ma kill that bitch!"

Suddenly Neil shouted, "Look at these niggas, man!" as he stepped back out of the jeep and started shooting from behind the jeep. Then Bo leaned across the back seat and grabbed one of the AK-47's, and some shots were fired back in the jeep. It was Damien, and the other fella running toward the jeep blasting with an assault rifle and a shotgun. Neil had run across the street and started shooting from behind a pickup truck which was riddled by the assault rifle. Bo slipped out of the jeep, ran around it to the street, and started letting loose.

Damien and the other guy took cover behind a couple of cars and continued to blast. Freddie hopped out of the jeep, got off a few rounds, and then made a run for his girlfriend's apartment. Damien rose up from behind a car and started blasting at him, and bullets flew through Freddie's body. Neil saw Freddie's body drop to the ground from behind the pickup truck. Neil stood up and blasted. Then Bo started blasting. The assault rifle was empty, so he sprinted across the street to Neil, grabbed him by the shirt and they both ducked into an alley. Neil shouted, "I dropped the gun!"

"Fuck that gun!" Bo shouted as they hopped a fence and kept running.

At the car wash Bruce said, "Damn, y'all heard that," as he, Champ, Busty, and Donkey stood under the fourth cover. After they came from Holly's house, they had heard the shots ringing out loud all the way at the car wash.

Donkey stated, "Them mutha fuckas over there is acting bad."

"Shidd!" Busty replied. "That sounded like it was around ya girl Que set or in the Melph or something," he added.

"No, indeed!" shouted Champ. "That was in Zane City probably."

"For real," added Donkey.

It was about five minutes later when a dope fiend named Hickey walked up to them and said, "I got seventy yards. Hook me up with two nice ones," as he held money out in his hand while looking around at everybody. Donkey looked at Bruce, who in turn was staring at the fiend.

Busty said, "Man, what y'all standing around looking crazy and shit for? Serve the man!"

Hickey said, "Yeah, my nigga, take care of me so I can get up!" Bruce walked toward the back to the stash, turned, and handed him two five-dollar balloons, and he started walking off. Then Hickey stopped, turned around, and said, "Say Lil' Penny Man, they getting kind of big, huh!"

Donkey replied, "That's a new package. You know how the fresh batch be."

Hickey said, "Yeah, I know!" and he left. They all stared at him as he disappeared into the night.

THE END
OF PART ONE

LOOK for LOYALTY, LOVE,

& BETRAYAL

**SURVIVING THE HAND THAT WAS DEALT
GROWING UP IN THE HOOD**

PART TWO

BY AUTHOR WAYNE GRIND - **COMING SOON!**

Wayne Grind

ABOUT THE AUTHOR

Wayne Grind is one of the hardest working men in entertainment. He is from Franklinton, Louisiana, and gained his start and name as a promoter in the entertainment industry. With the mentality to Network and Grind, he has put on several shows in different markets, working with various artists such as The King of Swing Tucker, Big Pokey, Juvenile, Yung Buck, Kelsey Nykole, Juicy Badazz, Karlie Red, and J Harden, just to name a few. He is CEO of WG Management/Consultant and Co-CEO of The Network Grind. His company The Network Grind is responsible for discovering rap artist Ed Da Realist from Richmond, VA. Wayne currently manages Super Producer Heartbeatz, and his company consulted with Lil' Boosie's mother while Lil' Boosie was incarcerated. Wayne Grind has a gift in discovering talent, and he loves to put people together to create something great. The Network Grind is a catalyst for the independent artist as well as a company that bridges people together for positive change, putting on different events for community, teens, and the homeless. The Network Grind has provided many Easter baskets for kids in high-risk neighborhoods, fed and clothed the homeless, as well as provided over 500 wigs for people suffering with cancer -- and that's only a few of the events his company has hosted.

Wayne's first love is for kids in high-risk neighborhoods. His mission is to teach the youth and guide them to a better way of life to prevent them from becoming a product of their environment. His goal is to send a strong message to help slow down the violence that has rapidly increased in many minority communities around the world. He doesn't use the phrase "Stop the Violence" because he realizes that before it stops, there has to be effective ways implemented to help modify the mentality of the youth. With consciousness and awareness, violence will decrease, resulting in high-risk neighborhoods being restored.

Mr. Grind was born and raised in Louisiana and throughout his youth, teen, and young adult life, he spent years in and out of trouble. After 13 ½ years in and out of jail, Mr. Grind decided enough was enough. Once he learned the right ways to deal with anger and found a love for God, he was able to implement positive change in his own life. He made it out to turn a negative into a positive, but unfortunately, his 13 year-old son wasn't as fortunate. His son lost his life to gun violence, hit by a stray bullet during a shoot-out between two people in his neighborhood. So the hunger to save kids is one of Mr. Grind's primary focuses. If he can help stop even one mother or father from getting the news of tragedy, he is aiming to do whatever he can. He has just completed his first two non-fiction novels based on his life called *Loyalty, Love, & BETRAYAL: Parts 1 and 2 – Surviving the Hand That was Dealt Growing Up in the Hood*. He is excited to give his testimony and to give hope to young black men or to anyone suffering like he did.

If you would like Wayne Grind to speak at one of your events, you can book him at waynegrindpublishing@gmail.com.

Made in the USA
San Bernardino, CA
06 September 2016